TWAYNE'S WORLD AUTHORS SERIES

A Survey of the World's Literature

Sylvia E. Bowman, Indiana University
GENERAL EDITOR

GREECE

Mary P. Gianos, Detroit Institute of Technology
EDITOR

Longus

(TWAS 96)

TWAYNE'S WORLD AUTHORS SERIES (TWAS)

*The purpose of TWAS is to survey the major writers
—novelists, dramatists, historians, poets, philosophers,
and critics—of the nations of the world. Among the
national literatures covered are those of Australia,
Canada, China, Eastern Europe, France, Germany,
Greece, India, Italy, Japan, Latin America, New Zea-
land, Poland, Russia, Scandinavia, Spain, and the
African nations, as well as Hebrew, Yiddish, and
Latin Classical literatures. This survey is comple-
mented by Twayne's United States Authors Series
and English Authors Series.*

*The intent of each volume in these series is to present
a critical-analytical study of the works of the writer;
to include biographical and historical material that
may be necessary for understanding, appreciation,
and critical appraisal of the writer; and to present all
material in clear, concise English—but not to vitiate
the scholarly content of the work by doing so.*

Longus

By WILLIAM E. McCULLOH

Kenyon College

Twayne Publishers, Inc.   ::   New York

ΤΟΚΕΤΣΙ

ΠΟΙΜΕΣΙ

LONGUS

by

WILLIAM E. McCULLOH

Daphnis and Chloe, despite its unpretentious and frolicsome surface, is the last comprehensive religious vision of life which pagan antiquity created in narrative form — its last *mythopoiēma.* The vision is presented through a unique pastoral-utopian version of the erotic romance. McCulloh's study attempts to show the allusive, eclectic richness of Longus' work, tracing its creative appropriation of various literary forms and traditions, especially those of the pastoral and the romance. The study concludes with speculation on the current and continuing importance of Longus.

ABOUT THE AUTHOR

William E. McCulloh holds B.A. de-
gress from Ohio Wesleyan University
and Oxford University (*Literae Humani-
ores*), and a Ph.D. in Classics from Yale
University. He has taught Classics at Wesleyan University and, since 1961, at Kenyon College. He is author of "Introduction" to *Greek Lyric Poetry*, translated
by Willis Barnstone (2d ed., Bantam
Books, 1967), and several articles, reviews,
and translations.

Preface

No book hitherto published has been devoted to a comprehensive literary discussion of *Daphnis and Chloe*. The present work aims to treat the major aspects of this Romance in the context of successive strands in the ancient literary tradition. It concludes with a personal assessment of Longus' importance from a rather eclectic standpoint. The abundance of quotation I have indulged in may find some justification in Longus' unusually compressed, elliptical synthesis of many elements in ancient literature and culture: the reader needs some actual taste of the *smörgasbord*, rather than merely chewing on a cardboard menu list of references.

There are works which I have been unable to consult.[1] Others I have seen only after the manuscript was essentially complete.[2]

For Greek names, apart from some very familiar ones, I have tried to approximate the Greek rather than Latinate spelling. "Longus" is, however, left Latinate since it is itself originally Latin. The use of the capital in "Romance," "Romantic," and "Romancer" is meant to refer specifically to the ancient genre in distinction to any wider meanings of the words.

All translations are my own, except where noted. For translations from verse I have usually retained line divisions, although my renderings are not metrical. I find that such division helps pace the reading (even of the eye) and focus the attention phrase by phrase in a way suitable to poetry.

An approximate rendering of the full Greek title of Longus' story would be *The Pastoral Matters Concerning Daphnis and Chloe*.[3] For convenience I use simply *Daphnis and Chloe*.

Presenting a paper on Greek Romance to the Kenyon Symposium in 1964 and reading *Daphnis and Chloe* with my advanced Greek class have helped my thinking. I am grateful for the criticisms of the manuscript offered by my wife and Jeffrey Henderson, alumnus. Nearly continuous residence for seven years in Gambier, Ohio—an artificially rural situation—has helped to train my mind on the pastoral ideal.

Contents

Chronology

No certain dates have yet been established for Longus, whose
only known work is *Daphnis and Chloe.* The preponderance of
scholarly opinion, however, regards it as highly probable that his
time was the latter part of the second century after Christ, or
the earlier part of the third century. Particular arguments are
based on: (1) the literary influence which, it is claimed, Longus
exercised upon the more securely datable Alkiphron; (2) linguistic style; (3) relation to a transient idyllic fashion in wall
painting; (4) purchasing power of the drachma (as evidenced in
Book III 28–32). Nothing is known of the biography of Longus. If
he was not a native of Lesbos—a possibility—it is from internal
evidence in the story at least probable that he was personally
familiar with the island. For a fuller summary of the above topics,
see the edition by Otto Schönberger.[1]

A.D.
112 Death of Dion of Prusa.
120 Death of Plutarch. Birth of Lucian.
138 Death of the emperor Hadrian. Accession of Antoninus Pius.
161 Accession of Marcus Aurelius.
180 Accession of Commodus.
193 Accession of Septimius Severus.
211 Accession of Caracalla.

Some authors active during the probable approximate period of
Longus' life:

Greek: Lucian, the Philostrati, Aelian, Alkiphron, Hermogenes,
    Athenaios, Clement of Alexandria, Origen.
Latin: Apuleius, Tertullian (author of *Pervigilium Veneris?*).

For the chronology of other Romances, see pp. 23–24.

CHAPTER 1

"Primitive Literature"

Do the demi-gods die? On this question I have heard a story from a man who was no fool nor liar. Some of you have listened to Aemilianus the rhetor. His father was Epitherses, a fellow townsman of mine who taught me grammar. This Epitherses told of sailing to Italy on a ship loaded with freight and passengers. In the evening, when they were off from the Echinad islands, the wind dropped and they drifted near Paxi. Most of those on board were still awake; many were still at their after-dinner wine. Suddenly they heard a voice from Paxi, someone shouting for Thamus, and they were amazed. Now Thamus was the pilot, an Egyptian, and most people did not know his name. Twice Thamus kept silence, but on the third time he answered the call. Then the person on shore shouted across, "When you get to Palodes, tell them that Great Pan is dead." At this everyone was astonished, said Epitherses. As they were discussing whether it was better to heed the voice or to stay clear of the matter, Thamus decided to sail on past quietly, if there was a breeze; but if there should be a calm, then he would speak out what he had heard. So when they reached Palodes, as there was neither wind nor wave, Thamus at the stern faced toward land and said, "Great Pan is dead." He had hardly finished when there was a great lamentation mixed with cries of astonishment—not just one voice, but a crowd. (Plutarch, *The Obsolescence of Oracles* XVII)

This famous passage has produced many echoes in later literature. Milton characteristically blended it with biblical reminiscences from Jeremiah in "On the Nativity":[1]

> The lonely mountains o'er,
> And the resounding shore,
> A voice of weeping heard and loud lament;
> From haunted spring, and dale
> Edged with poplar pale,
> The parting Genius is with sighing sent;
> With flower-inwoven tresses torn

The nymphs in twilight shade of tangled thickets mourn.
("On the Morning of Christ's Nativity: Hymn" XX)

But some eighty years after the death of Plutarch in A.D. 120, his
story of Pan's death received, in effect and perhaps also in intent,
its first literary response.[2] An enemy fleet has raided a coastal
region, carrying off flocks from the countryside, along with the
shepherdess Chloe, who is thus separated from her lover Daphnis:

> The commander of the Methymnaeans, after sailing more than a
> mile away, wanted to give his soldiers a chance to rest from the raid.
> There was a promontory curving out crescent-like into the sea, provid-
> ing more quiet anchorage than harbors do. He lined up his ships at
> anchor here, keeping them offshore so they would not have any trouble
> from the peasants, and gave his men over to undisturbed celebrations.
> With all their abundance of plunder they drank, sported, and mim-
> icked a victory feast.
>
> The day was just ending, and the carousing was trailing off into
> the night, when suddenly the land seemed to be all ablaze; they heard
> a surging splash of oars, like a great fleet. Someone shouted for the
> general to get the men armed, others called out other things, and one
> man seemed to have been speared: he lay like a corpse. The effect
> was that of a night battle, with no enemies visible.
>
> Such was their night. But the following day was even more dread-
> ful. The bucks and she-goats of Daphnis had berried ivy on their
> horns; the rams and ewes of Chloe howled like wolves. Chloe herself
> was seen crowned with pine. In the sea too, many were the wonders.
> The anchors stuck fast in the deep when the men hauled on them; the
> oars broke when they started to row; dolphins leaped out of the water,
> struck the ships with their tails, and broke up the planks. Above the
> cliff, beneath the summit, they could hear the sound of the pan-pipes.
> But there was no pleasure in *these* pan-pipes, it was like a terrible
> trumpeting. So they were in turmoil, ran for their weapons, shouted
> "Enemies!" when there was none to be seen, and prayed for night to
> come again in hopes of getting a truce then. Everyone who could think
> straight realized that the portents of sight and sound came from Pan's
> wrath against the sailors. But they could not think what wrong they had
> done—for no Pan-shrine had been plundered—until at midday the
> commander, under divine power, fell asleep and saw in a dream Pan
> himself, who said to him, "Why have you been so insanely reckless, you
> godless brutes? The countryside I love, you have filled with war; the
> herds of cattle, goats, and sheep in my charge you have driven off; and
> you have torn away from a sanctuary the maid whom Eros has chosen
> as heroine of his tale." (*Daphnis and Chloe* II 25–27)[3]

In addition to its reaffirmation of Pan, this passage in its last sentence suggests a religious motive for the whole work to which it belongs. In fact, *Daphnis and Chloe* is the last great literary formulation of the ancient pagan religious tradition. But it is more than this: it is the last great creation in pagan Greek literature. Such a claim must cope with a variety of critical objections. Not only can chronology be disputed and rival candidates for the honor be submitted. It is furthermore quite possible to argue that the book has been radically misunderstood if it is taken so seriously; it is in fact possible to argue that the work is instead a monument of sophisticated, decadent insincerity and spurious naïveté. These points will have to be faced in their time. And an even more thoroughgoing onslaught will have to be faced from the opposite direction: "The classics are only primitive literature. They belong in the same class as primitive machinery and primitive medicine" (Stephen Leacock, "Homer and Humbug").[4] Whatever the truth of this manifesto concerning the classics generally, such has been the reaction of many readers to Longus' "novel." And primitive indeed it may seem at first, to the reader who comes to it from a diet of modern novels, skims it rapidly, and retains only an impression corresponding more or less to the following summary:

Book I. On the island Lesbos near the city Mitylene, in the old days before Roman domination of Greece, and when there were still independent city-states,[5] a wealthy man had a country estate. One of his goatherd slaves, Lamon, found one day in an ivy-covered glade a goat suckling a baby boy. (One ancient Greek way of dealing with unwanted children was to leave the child in the country with tokens to identify it later, if need should arise.) Lamon took the baby home to his wife Myrtale; they agreed to rear it as their own son and named it Daphnis.

Two years later a shepherd-slave, Dryas, found a sheep suckling a baby girl near a fountain in a cave, shrine of the Nymphs. He took her to his wife Nape; they named her Chloe.

When Daphnis was fifteen and Chloe thirteen, Lamon and Dryas had the same dream in the same night: the Nymphs delivered the two children over to a winged boy, who then bade them become herdsmen, Daphnis a goatherd, Chloe a shepherdess. The dream-vision was obeyed; the two began to spend their days together in the pastures. It was spring and they passed the time in various childish sports, often imitating the play of the birds, bees, and lambs.

But a wolf had been troubling the flocks; shepherds had dug a pit to trap it; Daphnis fell into the trap while chasing a goat. In absence of rope, Chloe's breastband served to pull him out, unharmed but muddy. With Chloe he went to bathe in the spring at the cave of the Nymphs. As she helped him, Chloe was for the first time struck by Daphnis' beauty and thenceforth found her thoughts constantly taken up with him. But she did not understand what this new thing happening to her was.

Now it was Daphnis' turn: Dorkon, an oxherd, fell in love with Chloe and brought her gifts. One day he and Daphnis debated their beauty, with a kiss from Chloe as the winner's prize: Daphnis won, and Chloe's kiss had the same revelatory, mysteriously troubling effect on him as his bathing had had on her. Dorkon was a bad loser; he laid a rather improbable plot to dress up in a wolfskin, catch Chloe alone, and rape her in this curious incognito. But the sheepdogs attacked him as a wolf, and he had to call on the unsuspecting Daphnis and Chloe for help.

Throughout the summer the nameless passion of the pair grew amid their games. (In a brief digression, Daphnis one day told Chloe the story of the mourning dove—how it had once been a maiden tending cows.) But in early fall some Phoenician pirates raided the shore, carried off Daphnis with Dorkon's oxen, and left Dorkon dying. In his last moments the oxherd did the "far, far better thing" by telling Chloe the way to rescue the herd and Daphnis: play a certain tune on Dorkon's pan-pipes. At the sound of the music the oxen, out at sea, jumped overboard *en masse* and swamped the ship. The pirates drowned; Daphnis rode safe to shore between two oxen. Daphnis and Chloe then gave Dorkon ceremonious burial. Chloe bathed with Daphnis at the cave, so inflaming Daphnis that he felt like a pirate captive still, "for he did not yet know of the piracy of Eros."

Book II. After helping with the fall vintage, Daphnis and Chloe were again in the fields when an old man from the neighborhood, Philetas, paid them a visit. That very day in his garden he had met the god Eros, who appeared as a winged youth and declared he was watching over Daphnis and Chloe. Philetas had therefore come to bring this news to the pair, that they were in the god's power, and informed them that the only cure for Eros was "kissing, embracing, and lying down together naked." Upon reflection they agreed with Philetas' diagnosis of their condition and tried the cure. But their ignorance kept them from discovery of the right way to apply it.

And now another episode interrupted. A group of rich playboys on a pleasure cruise out from Methymna, another city of the island, anchored nearby and disembarked for a hunt. They had lost their hawser, so they used a green wicker rope as substitute. Daphnis' goats were frightened out of the hills onto the shore by the hunting, and one of them nibbled the rope in two. The unmanned ship was swept out to sea. The enraged playboys picked on Daphnis for this, but he was rescued by the neighboring peasants, who set up a trial with Philetas as judge. Each side presented its case; the verdict went to Daphnis; the Methymnaean youths rebelled and had to be beaten into flight.

When they got back to Methymna, to hide their disgrace the youths blamed Mitylene, not just the peasants, so a fleet was sent out for war. On the way it raided the local fields and, along with other plunder, tore Chloe away from her asylum in the cave of the Nymphs. For this the supernatural wrath of Pan was revealed to the fleet (see the passage quoted at the beginning of this chapter). They saved themselves from total destruction by releasing their spoils. To the music of mysterious, unseen pan-pipes Chloe marched home at the head of the restored flocks.

Daphnis and Chloe and their families held festivities in honor of Pan and the Nymphs, who had saved Chloe. In this they were joined by Philetas and his son Tityrus. Philetas agreed to display his mastery of the pan-pipes. (While Tityrus ran home to fetch his father's pipes, Lamon provided another digression with a story he learned from a Sicilian goatherd: how Syrinx—the Greek word for pan-pipes—was a girl chased by Pan; she vanished in the reeds of a swamp, and from those reeds Pan invented the pipes.) After Philetas' show of art, he played accompaniment to mimic dances of the shepherds, which Daphnis and Chloe capped by miming the story of Pan and Syrinx. Daphnis now tried Philetas' great set of pipes. Philetas was so charmed that he gave them, as master to star pupil, for Daphnis in turn to bequeath when he would be old. The next day Daphnis and Chloe took lover's oaths of each other.

Book III. Mitylene now marched out against Methymna, but

before battle could be joined, negotiations ended the pocket war.
Winter came on, and a heavy blizzard. Everyone was kept indoors. Daphnis and Chloe suffered the pangs of separation. The
more resourceful of the two, Daphnis, picked bird-catching as his
pretext and went to a favorable site, a thick patch of bird-food ivy
and myrtle berries near Chloe's hut. But no one came out, and he
could not think of an excuse for knocking, so he would have
waited all day in vain, if Dryas' dog had not chanced to run out
with a stolen piece of meat, his master chasing. On seeing Daphnis, Dryas invited him in for dinner. He stayed overnight and
joined the family next day in their winter Dionysus feast. In this
and similar ways Daphnis managed to visit Chloe during the
winter.

When spring returned, Daphnis' passion was hotter than ever,
especially at the sight of the mating animals. He tried to imitate
the rams and bucks with Chloe, but his ignorance still defeated
him. Enlightenment came at last in the person of Lykainion, the
young city-bred wife of an elderly neighbor. By a trick she got
Daphnis into the woods with her and showed him the "sought-for
path." But she also warned him of the pain and blood involved
for Chloe, as virgin, in her first time. Daphnis had been eager to
try out his new information on Chloe, but now, out of consideration for her, he decided to do nothing new. (When he rejoined
Chloe, the reverberation among the hills of songs from a passing
ship gave occasion for yet one more digression: the tale of the
maid Echo and her dismemberment by herdsmen whom jealous
Pan had frenzied.)

In the course of the summer many peasants came to Dryas and
Nape with proposals to marry Chloe. When Chloe warned him of
the danger, Daphnis sought the approval of his foster parents for
his own marriage to Chloe. From his rich birth tokens they in fact
considered him worthy of something better than a mere shepherd
girl. But to Daphnis they objected only that their own poverty
could give him no hope in the competition with his more wealthy
rivals.

The dejected Daphnis was cheered by a dream in which the
Nymphs told him to find three thousand drachmas washed up on
shore from a wreck. The spot would be marked by a dead and
malodorous dolphin. Daphnis found the purse next morning, and

with it won Dryas' consent. Dryas was then commissioned to persuade Lamon. Lamon found himself now without plausible objection and asked merely for postponement until the arrival of his master from the city in the fall: his master was the only one with authority for the final decision.

Book IV. With the approach of fall preparations began in full earnest to receive the master of the estate, Dionysophanes. Lamon gave special care to the master's elegant garden; Daphnis spruced up his flocks. But Lampis, one of Chloe's suitors, plotted to spoil Daphnis' chances of favor from Dionysophanes. One night he crept in, tore up and trampled the flowers of the garden. The peasants now expected the worst from their master. But providentially the master's son Astylos, an agreeable young-man-about-town, arrived several days ahead of time. He was persuaded to take their part.

So when Dionysophanes arrived, the matter of the garden passed off without trouble, and the master was delighted with everything else he saw; Daphnis too made a good impression. However, upon Gnathon, an aging urban debauchee who was the boon-companion toady of Astylos (the ancient term was "parasite"), he had, much against his wishes, been making only too good an impression. Gnathon soon managed to gain Astylos' support in asking Dionysophanes to give him Daphnis as his own plaything.

This new danger, when revealed to Lamon and Myrtale, brought on the denouement: Lamon showed the birth tokens to Dionysophanes, and Daphnis was joyfully discovered to be the latter's son. Amid the celebration Chloe seemed to be forgotten. Daphnis did not yet dare to speak of his love for her: such were the constraints of the class structure. So Lampis saw his chance and carried her off. But Gnathon also saw an opportunity to redeem himself in Daphnis' eyes; he took a band of men and rescued her. Under the circumstances Dryas decided the right time had come and gave over Chloe's birth tokens to Dionysophanes. The company returned to the city, where Chloe's true upper-class parentage was discovered through the tokens. The four foster parents were rewarded with liberty. The wedding was held in the country, in rustic style. And ever after, despite their rank, Daphnis and Chloe passed most of their time in the fields.

• • •

The above summary would serve very well to give an idea of
some ancient novels, and these would justifiably fall under Leacock's lash. But of *Daphnis and Chloe* the reader of summaries
will gain no idea at all. For example, even in this summary, perhaps two-thirds of the sentences will have been misunderstood
except by one who has some familiarity with Greek literature and
religion. The matter is analogous to the mishearing which must
inevitably occur when one listens for the first time to music of an
unfamiliar period or idiom.[6]

Above all the reader must not come to this book with the ex-
pectations which he brings to the traditional modern novel. He
must not look primarily for the depiction of individual personal-
ities in an acutely observed society as they work out their life-
problems. (The "realistic" novel is after all a phenomenon largely
of the past two centuries.) As a matter of fact, the reader attuned
to the *anti*-realist tendencies of the twentieth century is likely to
be in better shape for an encounter with *Daphnis and Chloe*. For
these anti-realist tendencies have in various ways deliberately re-
asserted myth over against historical reality, and *Daphnis and
Chloe* is the last Greek attempt at a formulation of existence in
mythical terms—a worthy Indian summer reminiscence of the
great phases of Greek creation through myth: epic, choral ode,
and drama. One literal version of the last sentence of the passage
quoted earlier on Pan's wrath would speak of Chloe as "a maid of
whom Eros wishes to make a *myth.*"

But this must be expounded later. For now, besides a mythical
orientation in the reader, there is an entirely different and most
extensive area with which he must make some acquaintance if he
is to attempt an adequate understanding of the book. To illustrate:
there is one basic feature of *Daphnis and Chloe* which I omitted
from the summary—the way it begins.

Longus starts by saying that he was once hunting in Lesbos, and
came across a picture painted in a grove of the Nymphs. He got
someone to explain to him what the picture was about and decided
to pass on the description to mankind at large. Now why is the
novel begun in this peculiar fashion? The answer is that Longus
is appropriating for his own purposes a Greek literary convention
—or rather, several of them, which we shall take up in their turn.

In fact the novel as a whole, as befits a tandem to the grand tradition, is a rich and subtle allusive composition of many memories and forms of that tradition. It could serve as the prime refutation of Leacock's claim that the classics are primitive. (I will not of course concede that it is always a vice to be primitive.) Few works of the twentieth century are, for better or worse, so cultivated.

Goethe in a famous laudation of Longus remarked, "One would have to write an entire book in order to do justice to all the great merits of this work." [7] But merely to reveal the full texture of the work—leaving evaluation to one side—would require that entire book, and a running commentary to the text as well. Anything like a full elucidation would take us too far into the intricacies of the Greek language, literature, religion, and culture. What I shall attempt in this book is simply to isolate most of the major ingredients of *Daphnis and Chloe* and suggest something of their composite effect—the total character of the work.

Most literary works, however complex, stand in closer relation to some one tradition than to any others. So for *Daphnis and Chloe* the first question is: What is that tradition? What sort of trunk supports the various ingrafted branches? For the answer we must turn to a consideration of that group of works known as the Greek Romances.

CHAPTER 2

Romance

THE Greek Romance was a form so late and of such undis-
tinguished rank that it was never assigned a separate genre
title by ancient critics. By those critics it was variously assimilated
to the recognized genres of epic, drama, and history. The term
"romance" is medieval in origin and was first applied to narratives
written in the Romance languages (as distinct from Latin), such
as those based on the Arthurian legends. With the rediscovery of
the ancient prose fictions in the Renaissance, the term was ex-
tended to some of these works as well.

There are many kinds of prose fiction in the ancient world.
Some of them present themselves under the mask of history or
biography (Xenophon's *Education of Cyrus*, Philostratos' *Life of
Apollonios of Tyana*). Some claim to be travel reports (Antonius
Diogenes, Iambulos). Some are a kind of short story (the "Mile-
sian Tales"—samples can be found in Petronius and Apuleius).
Taking Romance in its narrow and generally accepted sense, it is
however possible to isolate a genre of a distinct character. But
before giving a general characterization, here is a brief outline of
a particular, representative example which may serve to establish,
perhaps embed, the reader in the concrete:

Chaireas, the fairest young man in Syracuse, and Callirhoe, the
fairest maid not of Syracuse only, but of all Sicily, fall in love at
first sight during a public festival of Aphrodite. Their fathers
have previously been political enemies, but to save their children
from an obviously imminent death by languishment they agree to
a marriage. The many suitors of Callirhoe, naturally vexed at this
stop, contrive a revenge (identical with that of Don John in *Much
Ado About Nothing*): they arrange a scene to prove to Chaireas
that his bride has been cheating. Chaireas, young hot-head, runs
in and gives his wife a kick in the stomach without taking time

to find out the truth. The kick is apparently mortal, so Callirhoe is duly buried, and remorseful Chaireas resolves to commit suicide at her tomb at his earliest convenience.

But *meanwhile,* grave-robbers open the tomb and discover Callirhoe quite recovered. Off they go with her to the other end of the Mediterranean, where they sell her at Miletos as a slave. Her master, the noble widower Dionysios, at last persuades her to marry him. This otherwise unforgivable breach of Romantic etiquette on her part is justifiably motivated in the present case: Callirhoe has discovered that she is pregnant with the child of Chaireas and wants to assure free-born status for it.

In the meantime Chaireas has learned of Callirhoe's fate and sets out to recover his bride. Upon arrival, before he finds her, he is captured by the Persians and put to work in the mines.

Now it chances that the Persian satrap, Mithridates, comes to Miletos for a visit with Dionysios. Like everyone else he is greatly taken with the beauty of Dionysios' new wife. This is a piece of vast good luck for Chaireas. For the latter has inadvertently been implicated in a slave-revolt and is on the point of death by crucifixion when his connection with Callirhoe comes to the ears of Mithridates. This is enough to procure his instant release and adoption into the household of the satrap. It would be an immense oversimplification to say that the opposing claims of Chaireas and Dionysios to Callirhoe as wife are referred to the Great King of Persia himself for adjudication, but this is, more or less, what happens.

Expectedly, the king too falls in love with Callirhoe and postpones his decision in the case. When a revolt of the Egyptians calls him away, Callirhoe just accidentally happens to be included in his entourage. Chaireas joins up with the Egyptians, defeats the Persian navy, recovers Callirhoe, sails home to Syracuse, and tells the whole story to the assembled populace.

Such in outline is the earliest of the Romances which have survived entire. Its author is one Chariton, and it belongs to the first century A.D. or perhaps to the first century B.C. The occasional bilious flavor in my summary notwithstanding, the book can be vivid and absorbing, at least when one is in the right mood. There are five other Romances surviving complete (one in Latin, possibly a translation): Xenophon of Ephesos, *The Ephesian Tale,* ca. A.D.

100?; Achilleus Tatios, *Leukippe and Kleitophon,* ca. 172–194;
Longus, *Daphnis and Chloe,* latter half of second century? (see
Chronology); Heliodoros, *The Ethiopian Tale,* shortly before
A.D. 250; *anon.,* in Latin, *The Life of Apollonios of Tyre,* third cen-
tury at the earliest.[1] There are in addition fragmentary remains
of others.

In this group there are a number of more or less common features which can be isolated:

(1) Each Romance is, of course, a prose narrative.

(2) The subject matter is preponderantly (although not always
explicitly) fictional rather than mythical, legendary, or historical.
This characteristic sets Romance over against the vast majority of
ancient narratives, whether in prose or in verse.

(3) The fiction deals with a pair of lovers. The convention of
instantaneous passion is generally observed.

(4) A lavish series of external obstacles at once begins to unroll
to keep the pair apart. Some obstacles lie in the general category
of mischance: an intercepted letter, a storm at sea, or a band of
robbers. A Romance which fails to lead its pair at least from end
to end or top to bottom of the Mediterranean is usually loafing on
the job. Other mischances derive from counterpassions: the malice, illicit desire, or simply rivalry of some secondary characters in
the tale. Over and over, the beauty of the heroine—or of the hero
—proves its own worst enemy. Versions of Potiphar's Wife
abound.

(5) Through it all, the lovers manage to remain faithful to each
other—if not always literally so, at any rate faithful in spirit. In
general the hero and heroine, so far as they are characterized at
all, are thoroughly idealized.

(6) The unreality of the tale is further strengthened by the
absence of any clear historical setting. Most of the novels are
placed vaguely in the time before Alexander the Great. Persia is
still the great power in the East, and Greece is still a collection of
independent city-states.

(7) An indispensable feature of the ordinary Romance is the
theme of a divine Providence at work. There is usually one particular god or goddess prominent in the events, and at crucial
moments the divine intervention saves the day. The ending of a
Greek Romance is therefore invariably happy. (It is remarkable
that in three out of the six which have survived complete one of

the ruling divinities is the virgin-goddess Artemis, especially in her exotic, seemingly paradoxical form as the great mother-goddess at Ephesos. In accordance with the syncretist tendencies of later antiquity, this Artemis is sometimes further associated with the Egyptian goddess Isis.)

Greek Romance arrived late on the scene in ancient literature. It is in fact the last major Greek genre to emerge. In view of its lateness, it is not surprising that it incorporates a highly composite inheritance from the earlier literature. One of the great topics in classical scholarship for the past century-and-a-half has been the origin of Romance: Just how did all these peculiar features happen to combine? I do not propose to go into the history of the debate. It involves a very wide and detailed consideration of much ancient literature. The monumental and seminal work was Erwin Rohde's *Der Griechische Roman und seine Vorläufer* (*The Greek Novel and Its Antecedents*).[2] The book is now long superseded in its major conclusions, but still extremely valuable in the detail of its treatment. For the moment, two recent books in English seem to have come reasonably close to settling the question of origins, so far as it ever can be: Sophie Trenkner's *The Greek Novella*[3] and Ben Edwin Perry's *The Ancient Romances*.[4] My brief and imperfect account will derive largely from these works.

Perry gives a good warning: in any consideration of literary origins one should avoid thinking of antecedent forms as "causes" of a resultant genre.[5] The previously existing literary traditions could be conceived rather as a matrix upon which the imagination of the individual author imposes new conceptions. These new conceptions will at the same time comprise the author's response to his particular social-historical situation in the non-literary ("real") world. And here too the free initiative of the imagination is at work, so one should also avoid interpreting the relation between the author and his times in causal terms.

The question of origins may then, at least for purposes of simplification, be divided into two: What were the literary forerunners of Romance? And what was the social and historical situation to which it was in part a free response?

I *Forerunners*

The traditional way of exploring the origins of Romance has been to survey the existing *written* works in Greek literature and identify the various elements therefrom which seem to have been incorporated in Romance. For example, one points to those features of the *Odyssey*, of Greek drama, and of the historians which appear as anticipations. But thanks to Trenkner's slim, incisive volume, the account may now be put into a new focus.

It has been long established that behind the earliest written works in Greek literature, the epics of Homer, there lay an extensive period during which *oral* poetic composition was practiced. And oral storytelling in prose must also have existed in a variety of forms. But it remained for Trenkner to illustrate the way in which such storytelling persisted during the times of written literature, particularly at Athens during the fifth and fourth centuries B.C. She furthermore points out how the written Attic literature of this period appropriates and transforms the subject matter of these stories. The consequence for the origins of Romance is that much of the subject matter which was previously thought to have been derived directly from tragedy, history, and so on, can be seen instead to have sprung from this subsurface tradition of the oral tale.

But the picture thereby has become even more complex than before: from this soil of the popular oral tale various written genres sprang up, flourished, amplified and reshaped the folk material, and then passed away. Each of these written forms left its own mark on the subsequent written tradition. It therefore becomes difficult to separate the oral from the written contribution to Romance.

Since Trenkner has shown that all the basic ingredients for the subject matter of Romance existed already in the popular oral tale,[6] what *is* the indisputable minimum contributed by the written genres? Obviously, it must be the form and style, the treatment of the subject matter. Take the *Odyssey:* the long wanderings and mischances of Odysseus and his final reunion with Penelope (despite the malice of Poseidon and with the aid of Athena) are important for Romance above all in that they constitute the first large-scale dramatic structuring of that folk material which found its way also into Romance. Not all Romancers learned the lesson equally well, but the artistry shown in the disposition of their material by Heliodoros and Longus is testimony to this gift of Homer to subsequent literary craft. (Aristotle noted Homer's structuring power in a well-known passage in his *Poetics:* Chapter 8.)

But structure is not all. Homer is also the father of eloquence, and in the most basic way he stands behind the various forms of developed rhetoric deployed in the Romance. Beyond this, it was inevitable that various situations in a Romance would recall similar ones from Homer, in the mind of an educated reader. Chariton in fact is quite willing to quote a line or a phrase from Homer on suitable occasions: when Chaireas' mother begs him not to abandon her, she does so in a fashion which recalls Hecuba's entreaty to Hector in *Iliad* XXII, and Hecuba's own words are put in her mouth (Chariton II 5.6).

Another example is Euripides. He was the first to exploit erotic passion deliberately and fully in various forms as a dramatic subject.[7] Among his surviving plays the *Hippolytos* is probably the best illustration of this, with its portrait of Phaidra melting away in her unconquerable, adulterous passion for her stepson. But for all that, Euripides' contribution to Romance was not so much in the central exploitation of such passion in a plot (the oral story had done this) as it was in the psychological analysis and rhetorical expression of such passion, in the speeches and actions of the characters:

> How *could* I have ruined everything?
> What made me let go that way?
> I was crazy. It was a demon, hating me.
> Nurse, cover my head again.
> I can't bear to think of what I said.
> Cover me! You see these tears?
> I'm crying for shame!
> It hurts if I think straight.
> But when I'm mad, then I do something wicked.
> I want to die and go blank.
>
> (*Hippolytos* 239–49)

The rhetorical set pieces of the lover's soliloquy, whether newly love-struck, or despairing, or abandoned and outraged; the vivid depiction of the effects of passion—these are sure legacies of Euripides.

The relationship is tangled, to be sure: How is it possible to

estimate the degree to which Euripides influenced the subject
matter of Romance as well, in that he strengthened the taste of
the public for certain kinds of story? In any case, Euripides made
an undeniable impact on two other genres, both of which transmitted that impact to Romance.

For one thing, Attic New Comedy appropriated a number of
Euripidean features in plot and character which were passed on
to Romance; for example, the guiding divinity introduced in the
prologue (like Aphrodite in the *Hippolytus*, but now benign), the
tendency to treat the emotions of ordinary people seriously and
sympathetically, the employment of coincidence and surprise,
reversals and recognitions.

Another avenue of Euripidean influence was the writing of
history, which took an increasingly dramatic turn during the
fourth century B.C.; creation of pathetic effects, nurture of passion-
ate rhetoric, emphasis on erotic subjects—all helped to prepare
the way for a prose narrative which would favor these elements
while dropping any serious claim to convey information about the
past: Romance.

Along with the increasingly Romantic features, several other
developments in historiography should be mentioned for their
connection with Romance. Idealized, abundantly fictional biography became popular, especially Xenophon's *The Education of
Cyrus* and, later, sensationalist biographies of Alexander the
Great. The idealization of hero and heroine in Romance may
derive in part from this trend in historiography, although the full
explanation is doubtless more complex.

Another new trend was the proliferation of travel narratives,
whether for the purpose of serious geography and ethnography, or
of disguised ideology, or of simple entertainment. In one sense
this represents the strengthening of a taste for the exotic already
evident in the oral tale, and may therefore have helped to establish the Romance convention of abrupt peregrinations to all ends
of the ancient world. But some of these travel stories were put to
the service of philosophical utopian speculation: Iambulos, for
example, describes a fantastic communist Shangri-La in the Indian Ocean.[8] Now utopian literature can be found already in
Plato and in a sense goes back as far as Homer's Phaiakians.[9] But
its presence in the tradition of prose narrative helped to prepare
for that idealized setting which is a deliberately created feature

of *Daphnis and Chloe,* and which in smaller measure can be traced in at least one other Romance—in Heliodoros' picture of Ethiopia.

II   *The Propitious Times*

Enough for our purposes has now been said about the ingredients for Romance. To retain the specious metaphor of physical causation: What led to their precipitation into a single compound; what was the social and historical matrix? Two complementary factors may be traced. First, the decay of the circumstances favorable to the continued growth of the major genres of epic and drama: epic flourished during a period dominated by the aristocracy, and in the main it seems to have represented the world from the aristocratic viewpoint. (There are exceptions of course, Hesiod above all. But Homer pre-eminently represents epic, and the statement holds true for him.) This is not to say that an aristocracy is a sufficient condition for the creation of Homeric epic; it was, however, for Greece apparently a necessary condition: with the displacement of the aristocracy the creative mold was broken. Of course, Homer continued to be heard and read, but the major forms in which the societies of Greece found self-expression were thenceforth different.

One such form, particularly associated with the Athenian democratic city-state, was tragedy. But the close connection with the communal experience of a single *polis,* while constituting the special genius of ancient tragedy, also entailed the decline of the form when the *polis* as a major focus for human experience declined. This change began at the end of the fifth century B.C. and continued during the fourth. It was in large part the result of the defeat of Athenian imperial aims in the Peloponnesian Wars; the eventual aftermath of that defeat was the rise of the Macedonian Empire and the end of the independent *polis.*

So on the one hand, the withering away of epic (earlier) and tragedy (later) tended to leave a vacuum in the literary experience of the populace. At the same time, the populace which sought literary experience was growing larger and more cosmopolitan. During the fifth century B.C. the first circulation of books among a reading public began with the "publication" of dramas. The diffusion of an essentially Athenian culture—even beyond the traditionally Greek areas, thanks to Alexander's conquests—and the breaking down of dialect barriers through the formation of a com-

mon language, the *koinê*, meant that there was coming to be a
ready market for popular reading matter. This matter would in-
cline to be of a type which, in vulgarized form, would resume
those literary interests most readily exportable beyond the col-
lapsed boundaries of the city-state. The phenomenon is comparable to the demand for popular novels since the eighteenth century,
and indeed Perry (whose account I have been following) claims
a full parallelism between the factors operating in the rise of the
ancient and those of the modern novel.[10]

A concomitant of this change in the literary public was that it
became more difficult, if not impossible, to create works which
would seriously present a comprehensive vision of the world, now
that that world had so much enlarged, while losing much of its
previous focus. From what perspective was one to look out upon
the totality of things? The philosophers of course, by abandoning
a mythical-narrative formulation (apart from the occasional introduction of specially created myths, as in Plato), could achieve
a new kind of integration. But in narrative literature the thing was
done only rarely, and then with such inevitable complication,
sophistication, and allusiveness that it could never achieve the
mass currency that Athenian drama and Homer had enjoyed.

The following is a claim that should perhaps never be made
except in private; it shall nevertheless be made here in public:
After the fifth century B.C. only three narrative works (excluding
history) achieve an inclusive imaginative grasp of the world from
a pagan viewpoint: Vergil's *Aeneid*, Petronius' *Satyricon*, and
Daphnis and Chloe. All three were intended for a highly educated,
sophisticated audience, not for average readership. None of the
three came near to the spontaneous mass popularity which Homer
and Euripides had encountered among earlier audiences. (Aristophanes, for example, expects his Athenian crowd to catch all
sorts of sly comic Euripideanizing in his own plays.) To be sure,
Vergil became a school text, but this is hardly the same as mass
enthusiasm; mass acceptance would in any case be an anomaly
under the conditions of serious Latin literature. Only with the
advent of Christianity could "cosmic" seriousness once more characterize narratives for the masses. (For the full exposition of this
last thesis the reader should go to Erich Auerbach's *Mimesis*.)[11]

This is not to say that the popular novel presented itself

abruptly and openly as sheer entertainment literature. It was to be expected that it would still carry the husks left over from the serious genres to which it was related and for which it was to serve as some sort of substitute. Chariton's novel still has glimmerings of history: the heroine is the daughter of the famous Syracusan general Hermocrates, who figures in the pages of Thucydides, and the story itself is in part a disguised reworking of Syracusan legend.[12] Iamblichos' *Babylonian Tale* too is dressed up—packaged—as if it were a historical Romance. Such trifling disguises characterize the popular Romances.

In the case of authors who are aiming at a higher level of literary performance and reputation, the care—purely conventional though it might be—for the "wrapping" increases: Perry emphasizes that the ancient conventions never allowed full dignity to a work which was explicitly fictional; the taint of "mere entertainment" was apparently hard to avoid. So Longus takes his precautions; he provides for *Daphnis and Chloe* a characteristically complex and allusive costume. The book is first of all presented under the guise of an *ekphrasis,* or rhetorical-educational description. The *ekphrasis* was a genre that, once more, had its roots in Homer (the "Shield of Achilles," in Book XVIII) but had more recently acquired the status of an autonomous prose form (see Chapter 3 for more on this topic).

But *Daphnis and Chloe* is given additional external validation through association with historiography—and that by way of a most conspicuous literary reminiscence. At the end of his "Proemium" Longus says:

I formed [these] four books . . . to be a delightful possession for all men . . . one which will cure the sick and console the sorrowful; remind him who has loved and instruct in advance him who has not. For no one has ever escaped Eros entirely, nor ever will, so long as there is beauty and men have eyes to see it. But I pray the god to keep me sober as I depict others' passions.

The association with Thucydides seems to me unmistakable.[13] In his own declaration of intent the historian had said:

Perhaps its lack of entertaining stories will strike an audience as rather grim [literally, "rather undelightful"]. But some will wish to make a

clear inspection of the past and of that future which will, by virtue
of the human condition, resemble the past. If these men judge my
work useful, that is enough. It has been composed as a possession forever, not a showpiece for the moment. (I 22.4)

Longus repeats the key word "possession," reverses the role of
delight, keeps the instructional utility of the past for the future,
and adapts the justificatory principle of the perennial and universal recurrence of the subject chosen for analysis.

　　In view of the reference to cure, and the convention of erotic
passion as a sickness, there is also probably hovering here the
memory of Thucydides' equally famous words by which he mo-
tivates his description of the devastating plague at Athens:

Now each may speak of the probable source of it according to his own
knowledge, be he physician or ordinary citizen—including the causes
which in his view would be sufficient to empower a disruption of such
catastrophic magnitude. I shall simply describe it and point out those
marks whereby, if it should recur, a person might best recognize it. I
was sick with it myself, and witnessed the suffering of others. (II 48.3)

Longus too will describe a disease in the interests of medical
utility, and he too makes joint references to his own case and that
of others.

　　But this does not exhaust the ways in which Longus has made
overtures in the direction of history for the overt sanction of his
fiction. The story of the birth and rearing of Daphnis and Chloe
has clear associations with the "histories" of mythical and legendary figures, whether those of Zeus, Dionysos, and Hermes (where
the history is the religious history of myth) or those (originally
historical) of Cyrus and Alexander. For among other links with
divine or heroic "history" which Jack Lindsay and H. H. O. Chalk
have pointed out,[14] the births of Daphnis and Chloe are attended
by signs of supernatural favor—signs which recall, for example,
those involved in some versions of the birth of Cyrus:

[Harpagus] gave the child over to the shepherd of the royal flock
to be exposed. By chance a son had been born to the shepherd at the
same time. His wife, when she heard of the exposure of the royal in-
fant, begged that the boy be brought and shown to her. Yielding, the

shepherd went back to the forest and found beside the child a bitch-dog nursing it and driving off the wild beasts and birds. The dog's pity stirred his own. He brought back the child, with the dog anxiously following. When his wife took it in her arms, it played as if with its own mother. Such was its vivacity and sweet flattering merriment that the wife was led to ask the shepherd to exchange the two babies and expose her own.

(Justin, *Macedonian History* I 4)

(Compare the story of Romulus and Remus, which comes even closer to that of Daphnis and Chloe.)

Furthermore, Daphnis, whatever his apparent ordinariness, cannot be separated from the Daphnis who was the mythical son of Hermes and who became a sort of patron saint of shepherds. The story of Daphnis and Chloe is therefore on one level a playful imitation of the serious history of a legendary hero.

There is still more: reference has been made to purely fictional and quite fabulous travel stories, created in the interest of a philosophical message (the most important influence on these being Plato's myths). In a way to be spelled out more fully later, Longus' "idyllic" account of the love of goatherd and shepherdess must be regarded as a pastoral variant of the utopian philosophical tale. The connection may seem strained. But in fact, a missing link lies most conveniently to hand. In his *Euboean Discourse*, the rhetor and Cynic philosopher Dion of Prusa had already given a pastoral transmutation of the utopian philosophical travel story, with the intent of illustrating country virtue (and its overtones of the Cynic "life according to nature") over against city vice. It remained for Longus, while taking up and refining this simplistic contrast, to enrich the entire theme, not least by imposing the larger plot framework of erotic Romance.

These are the ways in which Longus, like the other literarily sophisticated Romancers (Heliodoros, Achilleus Tatios), provides protective coloration for his fiction. We now leave the consideration of the central trunk on which Longus' creation grows. Later on, some of the ways in which *Daphnis and Chloe* is distinguished from the standard Romance will be examined. But without some previous acquaintance with the standard Romance, much of the point of Longus' special achievement would inevitably have been missed.

I have just referred to a certain Dion of Prusa and his *Euboean Discourse*. The proper understanding of Dion and therewith of another entire literary sector of our novel, requires a chapter to itself.

CHAPTER 3

Euphues

Armado. I do affect the very ground, which is base, where her shoe, which is baser, guided by her foot, which is basest, doth tread. I shall be forsworn, which is a great argument of falsehood, if I love. And how can that be true love which is falsely attempted? Love is a familiar, love is a devil. There is no evil angel but Love. Yet was Samson so tempted, and he had an excellent strength; yet was Solomon so seduced, and he had a very good wit.

(Love's Labour's Lost I, ii, 172ff.)

Polonius. My liege, and madam, to expostulate
What majesty should be, what duty is,
Why day is day, night night, and time is time,
Were nothing but to waste night, day, and time.

. . . .

That he is mad, 'tis true. 'Tis true 'tis pity,
And pity 'tis 'tis true—a foolish figure,
But farewell it, for I will use no art.

(Hamlet II, ii, 86ff.)

Where did the Elizabethans acquire the fashion of this sugared style, here parodied by Shakespeare, with its short, artificially balanced phrases, manipulated series, and atomized rhythms? John Lyly is given the credit for its currency (through the influence of his novel *Euphues* and his plays), but Lyly did not invent; he appropriated, probably indirectly, from a particular classical rhetorical tradition, and one which is intimately involved in the ethos of at least half of the surviving Greek Romances.[1]

The popular Romance had always had rhetorical elements; such occasions for "heightened" prose as debates and love letters, already in Chariton, show this. But by the end of the first century after Christ a new wave of interest, a new craze, for rhetoric developed, particularly in the Greek-speaking section of the Roman

35

Empire, and partly as a consequence of the renewed interest in
Hellenic culture under Hadrian. The traditional name for this new
craze is the Second Sophistic.[2]

Rhetoric had for long been the culmination of the standard
educational sequence; students were set to work composing artificial speeches on assigned topics—"Should Cato commit suicide?"
(See Juvenal VII 150ff. for the miseries of the teacher who had to
listen to these things over and over.) Now a curious hypertrophy
of this practice occurred: professional speechmakers became extremely popular; such men would circle the Mediterranean,
eagerly sought after by a succession of cities. The excitement of
their arrival, and the crowds at their performances, could be paralleled today only by those which surround the celebrities of
sports and popular music (or perhaps poets, in Russia). Rohde
has given a famous description of such performances:

> Of the interaction between speaker and audience in such exalted
> moments it is difficult to get a true notion. One can however imagine
> that on such occasions the agreeable sense of his own powers which
> was aroused by the process of spontaneous creation, and the half-
> musical intoxication kindled by the sonic undulation of the speech-
> harmonies, actually carried the successful orator to a state of inspira-
> tion which the ancient rhetoricians compared with the *furor poeticus*—
> a not inapt comparison, in that such inspiration, despite its excitement,
> did not lose control of the carefuly practiced devices of craft.
>
> The whole person of the orator contributed to the performance of
> the rhetorical composition. The voice, strengthened by training and
> regimen, followed all the moods of the words with an almost musical
> expression, which sometimes, in a vice inherited from Asianic rhetoric,
> was distorted into actual song, and could, like bird-song or lyre-
> playing, delight even the hearer ignorant of Greek. The singing tone
> (which one can still today observe in a recitation of poetry which
> overemphasizes the rhythmic element) was perhaps assisted by the
> attention which ancient rhetoric bestowed on the rhythmic construc-
> tion even of prose, and which was developed to a degree of delicate
> sensitivity quite beyond the capacity of our modern ears.[3]

As a counterpiece to Rohde one should also look at the portrait
drawn by Synesios:

> How wretched is the lot of those who deliver show-speeches in
> the theaters! For it is impossible to please so many different sorts of

people at once, yet this is what the public speaker must attempt. He
is a communal slave, at the mercy of everyone; anyone who wishes
can spoil things for him. If someone laughs, the sophist [i.e., fancy
speechmaker] is done for; and he is suspicious of a solemn face, for,
no matter what sort of speech he is putting out, he is after all a
sophist and is scrounging around for glory, not true assessment. He is
also bothered by a person who pays close attention, as if looking to
catch him in a fault; but it is just as much trouble to have someone
turning his head away in all directions, as if thinking the speech is
not worth listening to.

You would suppose he were on trial before harsh masters, the way
he has spent so many sleepless nights, and racked himself for so many
days, nearly draining the life out of himself from hunger and anxiety,
in order to scrape together a good speech. And here he comes, bearing this sugared, pretty speech-gift to his haughty sweetheart—the
crowd which has worn him out, although he pretends to be in the
pink. He got himself bathed in advance of the great day and shows
up with an elegant costume and bearing (he must *look* well too);
smiles at the crowd and seems happy, but inwardly he is tied up in
knots—he has even eaten tragacanth to make his voice clear and
penetrating.

Not even the proudest of such men would deny that he is concerned about his voice and has taken pains with it. He even turns
aside in midspeech to ask his servant for the flask, and the servant
hands it to him—it has been gotten ready long ago—and he takes a
swallow and gargles, so as to make a fresh attack on his word music.
But not even so can the poor wretch propitiate his hearers: they are
hoping his voice will break, so they can laugh. They would even like
for him to open his mouth and raise his hand, like a statue, and then
stand there more speechless than a statue. That way they could go
home, which is what they have been wanting to do for quite a while.

(Synesios, *Dion* XII 54d–55d)

The effect of the Second Sophistic oratorical mania on Greek
Romance can be divided into two main sections: the style, and the
subjects upon which the style was exercised.

I *Style*

The effect of the Second Sophistic movement was to revive not
merely a general cultivation of things rhetorical, but also the specific rhetorical tendency known as Asianism. Asianism was a complex of various elements, but its basic character was that of
extravagance and affectation. The grandfather of Asianism was

the fifth century B.C. sophist Gorgias, and the following passage
from his funeral oration gives a fair idea of what Asianism in one
form was capable of:

What was absent to these men of the things which should be present
to men? And what was present of the things which should not be present? (May I be able to say what I wish, and may I wish what I should,
missing divine anger and escaping human envy.) For these men possessed a virtue that was godlike, but a mortality that was human,
often preferring mild equity to stubborn justice, often to legal pedantry
rational aptness.

      (Diels-Kranz, *Die Fragmente der Vorsokratiker*, Gorgias, fr. 6)

    To Asianism was opposed another stylistic tendency known as
Atticism. The Atticist cultivated—together with an Attic (classical
Athenian) vocabulary, morphology, and syntax—also the virtues
of naturalness and harmony. But Greek Romance was inundated
by Asianism. How apt a fusion this was has been formulated in a
brilliant page by Samuel Lee Wolff:

Here indeed the loose structure and the flashy style fit each other. The
loose structure requires the reader to leap in thought from an X to a Y
that is not essentially connected with it: expecting more of X or its
consequences, he is suddenly confronted with Y, and his expectation
defeated. The flashy style, where X—which the reader never thought
was Y at all—is said to *be* Y, or where X and Y—which the reader
had been associating—are suddenly dissociated and opposed, is partly
the fitting expression of such cheap relations between things, their ir-
relevancy, their haphazard connections, their violent severances—and
partly deliberate claptrap. Structure and style alike convey a base view
of life and of the function of literature. So far from seeking to unify the
divers phenomena of life under law, the Greek Romance prefers to
keep them apart, in all their chance diversity, showiness, and separate
sensuous appeal. Law, permanency, consistency, the unity in spirit of
that which in matter is so various and contradictory—all this is too
sober, too dull. Let us have what is truly interesting; let us have what
moves and jingles and glitters. Let us have the passing show.[4]

If Wolff's remarks are applied to *Daphnis and Chloe,* his estimate
of its ethos is totally misleading. But he strikes close to center for
other Romancers. It is time to sample. Here are two contrasting

sorts of morbid excess which may be found in Romance. I shall
nickname them Rococo and Baroque.

Rococo:
Much was the display of incenses; much the interweave of flowers. The
incenses: cinnamon and frankincense and saffron; the flowers: jonquil
and rose and myrtle. The perfume of the flowers strove with the aroma
of the incenses.   (Achilleus Tatios II 15)

Bring the wheel; here are my hands: stretch them. Bring whips too;
here is my back: strike it. Bring fire; here is my body: burn it. Bring
a sword too; here is my throat: slit it.   (Achilleus Tatios VI 21)

Baroque (I resort to typography to assist the reader):
When they thought they were safe for the present and were passing
the time peacefully, at about midnight A CERTAIN PART OF THE DIKE,
where in the evening the Ethiopians had begun to dig—*whether* it
was because, after the earth was loosely and lightly piled up at that
spot, the portion underneath gave way when wet, *or* because the un-
derminers provided an empty space for the dirt to shift into, *or* because, after the shallow trench was made by the diggers, the water
rising during the night overflowed and, a path once broken through, it
grew deeper, *or* one might call it the work of divine assistance—
UNEXPECTEDLY BROKE OUT.   (Heliodoros IX 8)

Where Plato and Demosthenes have the power to inform a long,
complex sentence with dramatic tension and variety throughout
(thereby achieving unparalleled intensification at climactic moments), Heliodoros is here—and often—simply grotesque in his
extravagance. As one translator says, "Heliodoros loves phrases for
full orchestra. Unfortunately there is no music to accompany
them." [5]
    It is not always possible to classify neatly the style of a given
author as Atticist or Asianic. Longus has been certified by Gunnar
Valley as an Atticist in his diction. [6] But in his rhetoric the matter
is more complicated. In the purely narrative passages, Longus
often writes a Greek which—especially for his time—was remark-
ably simple and straightforward. But in descriptive passages and
in speeches he cultivates a highly Rococo form of the Asianic. The
following may serve for a sample anatomy (I shall incorporate
analytical guide marks):

It was spring's beginning,
and all flowers were burgeoning,
   some in the woods,
       A
   some in the meadows,
       B
   and those of the mountains.
       C
Already there was buzzing of bees,
          1   I
       singing of musical birds,
         2   II
       frisking of newborn lambs.
         3   III
The lambs frisked in the mountains,
  III   3   C
in the meadows buzzed the bees,
  B   1   I
the copses birds filled with song . . .
  A   II   2

[Daphnis and Chloe], when they heard the birds singing, sang; when
they saw the frisking lambs, pranced nimbly; mimicking the bees, they
gathered flowers.   (I 9)

The above passage is built on the tricolon, or group of three
phrases. There are four tricola. The first three are cumulative, with
deliberate artifice in the varied order of components (as indicated
by my markers). In addition to all this "passing show," other passages employ rhymes at the ends of parallel phrases. See for example the passage from I 23, which I have tried to approximate
on p. 72. And the Asianic fondness for word play betrays itself
in Longus by several notable puns.[7]

   How is one to respond to such a style? Many—Rohde above all
—have regarded it as a centrally damning feature of the work,
prime evidence of Longus' corruption and insincerity.[8] But thanks
to our position in the literary stream it is perhaps more possible
for us to appreciate the virtues—even the seriousness—of stylistic
artifice. Above all, the reader should be fully open to the "third
dimension," the spoken sound of the text, to which William Arrowsmith has drawn attention for all ancient novels.[9] (For that
matter, all artistic prose in the ancient world was meant to be

heard; the ordinary reader understood each word of a text by pronouncing the syllables, not by visual recognition.)[10] This third dimension exists of course for most modern novels also, but the general reading public now has to be specially reminded of it. When this sonic dimension is perceived in Longus, the artificial, flutelike arabesques of his prose music are in full harmony with his general literary intentions, which are something more than rustic realism, and something better than the meretricious virtuosity (laid bare by Wolff) of most Romantic rhetoric. Of these intentions the full discussion must be reserved for later. But I would particularly urge that the reader be alert to the notes of playful irony and glancing parody in the purple passages. It is part of the Mozartian ambivalence of *Daphnis and Chloe* that its seriousness is everywhere salted with sport.

II *Subjects*

To the professional orators of the Second Sophistic and to their audiences the stylistic performance was what counted, not the subject upon which the orator's brilliance was exercised. In principle, then, any theme could serve as a point of departure, as, for instance, in Lucian's "Praise of the Flea." But in practice certain types of subjects tended to predominate, for the ease with which they lent themselves to rhetorical development. Among those which made their influence felt in the Romances were:

(1) Formal speech genres, such as deliberations (*suasoriae*), argumentations (*controversiae*), and lamentations. A number of these types, transposed into the mode of pastoral simplicity, can be found in *Daphnis and Chloe*: *suasoria*—Daphnis trying to decide whether to knock at the door to Chloe's cottage, III 6; *controversia*—the court speeches of the Methymnaean youths and Daphnis, III 15–16, or the debate of Dorkon and Daphnis, I 16; lamentation—Lamon over the ravaged park, IV 8.

(2) Formal lecture, pretending to convey information on a given topic. In Heliodoros and Achilleus Tatios one may find many portentous digressions of this sort. Their equivalents in Longus are the several etiologies interspersed in the narrative; that is, stories purporting to explain the origin of something—pan-pipes, or the echo, or the moaning of the dove. Although these stories derive also from the Hellenistic poems on metamorphoses (as

does Ovid's *Metamorphoses*), they are at the same time sportive pastoral variants of conventional Romance encyclopedism.

(3) Most important for the basic orientation of the work as a whole (see pp. 31, 81f., and 102): the formal description, or *ekphrasis*. This genre was so warmly welcomed that a probable younger contemporary of Longus, one of the Philostrati, put together an entire book of descriptions of paintings—the *Icons* (or *Imagines*)—and Goethe found it of sufficient interest to make a translation of it. One *ekphrasis* by a professional of the Second Sophistic (likewise a probable contemporary of Longus) indicates the presence of a taste for country scenes like those in Longus:

Let me now also depict and give form in speech to the Thessalian vale called Tempe. (For it is conceded that speech, when used with descriptive ability, can make an exhibit of what it wishes to with no less power than experts in the plastic arts.) Tempe is a place situated between Olympus and Ossa, which are lofty mountains separated as if by divine plan so as to allow a middle room. Its length extends to five miles, while its width is in some places a hundred feet, and in others a little less. The river Peneios flows down the middle. Other rivers join it and, by adding their streams, make it large.

This spot has the most varied sorts of attractions, not the work of human hands, but the result of nature's spontaneous ambition for beauty at the time when the place first came to be. For ivy burgeons there in dense abundance, creeping up and mingling with tall trees, like noble vines. Plentiful yew ascends the slopes and overshadows the rock. So the rock is hidden, while the sight of all the greenery is a feast for the eyes.

On the level ground below, there are various groves and continual covered patches—for summer travelers, delightful stopping places and good for cooling off. Many fountains spring up along the way, so that little chill refreshing streams are close by. The water is said to be good for bathing and even to possess medicinal virtues. There is also the sound of birds scattered throughout, especially of the songbirds—a treat for the ears and a pleasant escort for the trip, since the melody dissolves the weariness from the wayfarers.

Such are the charms and refreshments on both sides of the river, while in the middle of the valley the Peneios passes, advancing mild and smooth like oil. The shade from the pendent branches of the trees along the edge, reaching out over the river, blocks off the sun and makes the sailing cool.   (Aelian *Miscellany* III 1)

At the end of the preceding chapter we proposed to return to Dion of Prusa. Dion was a practicing Second Sophistician who was converted from rhetoric to philosophy—of an eclectic variety but with a strong Cynic cast. In his *Euboean Discourse,* Dion puts both rhetoric and ruralism to work for his philosophy. The Cynics, amid their diversity, were united in advocating a life of natural simplicity, divorced—inwardly, if not always outwardly—from the corrupt artificiality of the city. The *Euboean Discourse* fictionally describes how Dion was shipwrecked on the Euboean coast in the wilds. By chance he met a hunter who gave him shelter in his home and thereby also gave him opportunity to observe an "idyllic" style of life. The following quasi-*ekphrasis* will suggest the links with both Aelian and Longus:

The place is flanked by rises, a deep and shady gorge, and through the middle a gentle river, most suitable for cattle and calves to wade in. The water is plentiful and pure, since its spring is nearby, and a breeze blows continually through the gorge in the summer. The surrounding woods are open and well-watered—no breeding ground for gadflies and other cattle-bane. There are many fine meadows spread out beneath scattered tall trees, filled with grass all summer long, so there is no need to search for pasturage.

(Dion of Prusa, *Seventh,* or *Euboean Discourse* 14–15)

The hunter tells how he was once forced to make the long trip into the city and how he there encountered the degeneracy of the urban mob, the corruption of city life.

For his narration, Dion adopts a style of the utmost simplicity, quite at variance with the involved (and standard) syntax of the remainder of the oration. Despite the simplistic idealization of the tale, it has real attractiveness. But more important for our purposes, it prepares us for some of the significance which pastoral life will be given by Longus, who wrote some one hundred years later.

Furthermore, it gives us the clearest notion of any Greek writing I have yet come across from this period of the cultural situation in which Longus probably wrote. The time was very likely the tranquil age of the Antonines, or their immediate aftermath, and this was the period during which, as Gibbon is regularly quoted, "the condition of the human race was most happy and prosperous." [11] But even at this time the social and economic decay of many cities in the Greek area of the Empire was an accomplished fact:

Money was concentrated in the hands of a few. A total change of manners ensued: the rich became luxurious, the poor hardened, and the sharpest lines between classes were drawn. The rich were forced to bear the burdens of the government and to subsidize the poor in order to keep them in check. Election to office meant misfortune if not ruin. On the other hand, the common people, dependent on these subsidies, had become idle, restless, and greedy.[12]

This situation gives power to the special form in which Longus presents the city-country contrast. It is not simply the private peace and innocence of the country against the public bustle and evil of the city; this was as far as earlier treatments of pastoral themes took it. Witness, for example, Horace's *Second Epode:*

> Happy the man who, far from the press of affairs,
>   Like the bygone race of men,
> Works ancestral fields with his oxen,
>   Not tangled up by loans,
> Not shaken by the savage soldier's bugle,
>   Not shuddering at the angry sea:
> He is free of the forum and the proud thresholds
>   Of over-mighty fellow citizens.
>
> (Epode II 1–8)

(Horace, it should be noted, has other matters at work in this poem as well, which it is not to our present purpose to discuss.) For Longus the new element in the contrast is the emphasis on the divinely regenerative health of the country against the spiritual exhaustion of the city. Only the first half of this latter contrast is directly developed in the novel; for the second half there is merely the hint contained in the fact that economic stress forced even a leading citizen of Mitylene to expose his only child (IV 35). "One exposes a daughter even if one is wealthy," says one poet.[13]

With the city-country contrast and its expression in part by way of *ekphrasis*, we reach the last, the most intricate, and the most

important component in Longus' narrative. For the celebration of
the countryside did not begin with Dion, and the *ekphrasis*—although at bottom one more of Homer's progeny—is employed by
Longus in a way pre-eminently conditioned by one particular literary school. To that school we must now turn.

CHAPTER 4

Green Thoughts

IN a broad way the pastoral impetus can be discerned even at
the beginning of Greek literature, and even there it manifests
the two complementary aspects which we shall find in *Daphnis
and Chloe*. Those aspects are: paradise and pasture. Paradise is
simply the Greek word for pleasure garden (or park), particularly the royal pleasure garden of the Persian king. In the *Odyssey*,
although the word itself does not occur, its substance can be seen
in the following description of the palace of Alkinoos:

> Outside the courtyard near the gate
> was a large garden fenced in all round.
> Here tall trees abounded:
> pears, pomegranates, and apples with splendid fruit,
> sweet figs and flourishing olives.
>
> . . . .
> Here grow all sorts of trim herb beds
> at the foot of the row, radiant all year long.
> And two fountains, one flowing throughout the garden,
> the other at the courtyard's threshold rising toward
> the tall house. . . .
>
> (*Odyssey* VII 112ff.)

Thanks to the Epicureans, the garden was later to become an
explicit symbol of a particular style of life: one withdrawn from
the press of urban and worldly affairs, devoted to the harmonious
and intelligent enjoyment of simple pleasures; and the Epicureans
came to be called the Philosophers of the Garden. But the several
gardens of Longus, as we shall see, have a wider and more primordial symbolism than the Epicurean.

The other aspect of the pastoral, the pasture, appears in the
Odyssey in the Eumaios episode (Book XIV): the simple, whole-

some life of the stalwart, steadfast swineherd. The picture is not at all what it would later become, but even here there is an inescapable contrast between the honest countryside and the debauched, treacherous town. (I am speaking of the net effect of the opposed scenes, an effect which comes through despite the fact that there are evil herdsmen and faithful urban servants in Homer.)

It was to take four or five centuries, however, before an idealized pastoral existence could become the central subject of an entire school of poetry. It is hard to say just when country life begins to make a special appeal to the literary imagination. For the serious Athenian of the fifth century B.C. any ideal focus for life other than the city was unthinkable, unpatriotic. However, in various ways, Euripides and Aristophanes began to loosen the urban ties. Euripides had a study-retreat on the island of Salamis, and was thought odd for his reclusive ways. In his plays a noble peasant can excel all the other persons of a drama: witness the *Electra*. Aristophanes in several plays gives sympathetic voice to the country citizens, and even anticipates the pastoral style in such things as the following from the *Peace:*

> When the cicada sings its pleasant tune,
> I enjoy inspecting the vines of Lemnian grapes
> to see if they are ripe yet
> (the shoots come out early),
> and watching the swelling figs.
> Then when they're ripe
> I start munching away
> and praising the crop
> and crush the thyme to fix myself a drink.
> (Peace 1159–69)

Frequently in Aristophanes' peace-plays the joys of peace are assimilated to country pleasures. It is worth speculating that the true pastoral ideal began as an obsessive nostalgia among the crowds of Attic citizenry cooped up during the Peloponnesian Wars inside the city walls, barred from their countryside during the times when Spartan infantry marched unopposed through the land.

Even more important as a document of the sort of growing

pastoral sensibility which was to culminate in Longus is Plato's
Phaidros, with its setting which, for Plato, is so unusual, and of
such rich significance for the dialogue as a whole:

> *Socrates:* A lovely spot for a rest, by Hera! This plane tree is tall
> and leafy; the agnus too, and its blossoms are at their peak: the place
> is full of their scent. And here is a charming spring under the plane
> tree; I'll just sample its chill with my feet. Judging from the figurines,
> we must be at a shrine for Nymphs and Acheloios. And would you
> notice the delicious sweet breeze here! It makes a summer flute music
> to go with the cicada song. But the real treat is the grass: see how it
> swells out on this little slope for me to pillow my head. My dear
> Phaidros, you have simply outdone yourself with the arrangements!
>
> > (*Phaidros* 230 b–c)

Apart from the special purposes and experiences of individual
authors, there are two complementary factors which may be
adduced to account for the fact that a serious pastoral ideal became possible for literature. In the first place, as mentioned earlier
in connection with the development of Romance, the city lost its
focusing power for the moral existence of the citizen. But sec-
ondly, the restraint and inhibition of city life (for what reasons—
increasing size? increasingly conventional-bourgeois behavior?
failure of politics to preoccupy and distract?) produced a dialectical mirror image of free and natural life in the countryside,
particularly freedom in the relations between the sexes. Women
in the city were kept for the most part in a kind of purdah. Occasions for romantic attachments, apart from those with professional
party girls, were hard to come by; hence the prominence of encounters at holiday festivals in the plots of New Comedy. But
shepherds and shepherdesses—at least in the mind of the frus-
trated "white-collar" urbanite—possessed a wholly admirable
erotic freedom.

Although he is referring to a different age, the following passage by Johan Huizinga can serve as a general formulation of the
pasture form of the pastoral trend:

> For the most part the praises of a frugal life and of hard work in the
> fields are not based on the delights of simplicity and labour in them-
> selves, nor on the security and independence they seemed to confer;

the positive content of the ideal is the longing for natural love. The pastoral is the idyllic form assumed by erotic thought. Just like the dream of heroism which is at the bottom of the ideas of chivalry, the bucolic dream is somewhat more than a literary genre. It is a craving to reform life itself. It does not stop at describing the life of shepherds with its innocent and natural pleasures. People want to imitate it, if not in real life, at least in the illusion of a graceful game. Weary of factitious conceptions of love, the aristocracy sought a remedy for them in the pastoral ideal. Facile and innocent love amid the delights of nature seemed to be the lot of country people, theirs to be the truly enviable form of happiness. The villein, in his turn, becomes an ideal type.[1]

It is now time to take up the particular genre which became for Europe (until Renaissance mutations) the pastoral form par excellence: the bucolic poem, whose apparent inventor was Theokritos. More than any other author, it is Theokritos who has influenced the special character of Longus' Romance, so that it is the unique ancient example of what in the Renaissance was to become practically a genre of its own, the Pastoral Romance.

Theokritos—even in the pastoral portions of his work—is himself a complex phenomenon, as Gilbert Lawall's recent remarkable study has thoroughly illustrated.[2] From his "simple" pastorals IV, V, and VI (as contrasted with the more obviously mixed forms in I, III, and VII), V may serve as a starting sample: a pair of herdsmen is introduced, one a shepherd, and one a goatherd; they quarrel and propose a singing contest; a third is invited to judge, and at the end a prize is awarded. (This sort of contest, or agon—a version of the antiphonal or amoebeic verse associated with pastoral—recurs in *Daphnis and Chloe* when Dorkon and Daphnis contest for the prize of Chloe's kiss.) During the introductory conversation, details descriptive of the scene are slipped in; the songs themselves contain an abundance of reference, within conventional limits, to the detail of the herdsman's life; the vegetation, the animals, the clothing and equipment, the erotic trivia. A central convention is that of herdsman as poet and lover. The following dialogue between Komatas and Lakon will give some notion; it is taken from the agon:

K: The Muses love me much more than songster Daphnis:
not long ago I gave to them two kids.

L: Apollo really loves me much: I graze a ram
   for him, and the holy day is near.
K: But I milk two goats, each with twins,
   and that girl watches and says, "You don't want to
      milk alone, do you?"
L: Rubbish. Lakon crams cheese into twenty baskets,
   and tups the stripling among the flowers.
K: Klearista throws apples at me when I drive the goats
   past, and makes sugary chirps to call me.
L: And I've got slim Kratidas to drive me crazy when he
   comes by, waving that smooth hair around his neck.
K: But you can't class daisies and dandelions with
   roses in their rows along the fence.
L: No more can you put acorns with apples.
   Those have shells; these are honey.

(Theokritos V 80–95)

How did Theokritos arrive at this form? How, in particular,
do we suddenly find herdsmen, often slaves, at the center of
attention? Slaves and countrymen to be sure have figured in
antecedent Greek literature, particularly Comedy, but never
centrally. Further, how is it that so much of the interest of the
poem has come to reside in the artful serving up of homely detail? For part of the answer we should look at several other of
Theokritos' *Idylls* ("little forms"); more than half of his work
lies outside the pastoral class. The *Fifteenth Idyll*, "The Women
at the Adonis Festival," is a good example. One woman, Gorgo,
calls on another, Praxinoa. She steps inside when the maid answers the door, and asks:

G: Is Praxinoa at home?
P: Gorgo darling, it's been ages! Yes, I'm here.
   I'm surprised you made it. Eunoa, get a chair.
   And bring a pillow too.
G: Now don't bother about me.
P: You *must* sit down.
G: What a mad fool I was! I barely got here,
   Praxinoa, what with all that mob and those chariots.
   Boots everywhere, royal guardsmen everywhere,
   and the distance is frightful. Each time you
   keep on moving farther out!
P: It's that nut of a husband. He goes out to the rim

of the earth and buys a hole, not a house, just so we
can't be neighbors—out of sheer spite, as usual.
G: You shouldn't talk that way about him while the
child's listening. See how it's looking at you!
Don't worry, Zopyrion, you little sweetheart—
she's not talking about daddy.
P: Why the child *does* notice, would you believe it!
G: Nice daddy.
P: Yes, that nice daddy—you know what he did yesterday?
I say to him yesterday, "Papa, could you get me some
soap and some rouge from the store?" And he came
back with five pounds of salt, the big idiot!

(Theokritos XV 1–17)

After a bit the two women set out through the crowded city
streets to Ptolemy's palace to see the Adonis show (something
on the order of an Easter sunrise service). The piece ends with
the ritual song of the festival. The interest of the Idyll as a whole
is centered in the piquancy of the everyday detail of the per-
sonalities and the setting.

The form of which Theokritos here presents a highly polished
example was known to the ancient world as the mime. Mime was
a minor branch of drama. Instead of developing elaborate plots
and weighty themes, it contented itself with short scenes or a
series thereof; its usual interest (although in its vulgar forms it
could involve sensational action and melodrama) was in pro-
viding a vignette, purely for its own sake. Sometimes, however,
there were satirical overtones, for which compare the skits of
Mike Nichols and Elaine May. Among the remains in Greek there
are mimes on such topics as the following: an adulteress tries to
get rid of her husband; a young girl is questioned by her family
about a secret love affair; a mother brings her scamp of a son to
the schoolmaster for a whipping.[3] In short, the mime is one of
the very few classical literary forms which approximated a realistic style.

But in the mimes of Theokritos it is important to note a special
modification of the realism, important because the modification
will be transmitted to Longus; in Theokritos there is a conscious
artfulness in the selection and presentation of the detail. A part
of the interest is subtly deflected from the realism to the craft
whereby the realism is encased in art (a fly in amber). When

Praxinoa scolds her maid, the charm is sought through the perfection with which the colloquialisms are exquisitely frozen into
hexameter verse, that hexameter which hitherto had been chiefly
the vehicle of epic narrative. This refined dissonance between
subject and treatment is deliberately arranged. So when Theokritos transports the mime into the countryside, one should keep
in mind that the same modulation of realism persists: the rural
detail is wrought into a selective cameo miniature in which a
delicate incongruity is to be cherished. In the passage quoted
earlier from the *Fifth Idyll* consider the improbably deft sophistication of these verses in the mouths of herdsmen. The effect has
some analogies to the poetry of the French Parnassians and de-
votees of *la poésie pure.*[4]

We may seem to have gotten rather involved already in the
tangle of the pastoral style. But more is to come. Thus far we have
sampled only the "simple" pastorals of Theokritos. Another class
we might call the ironic or complex pastorals. In III, for example,
a shepherd serenades a flighty shepherdess who peeps from her
cave—quite straightforward stuff one might say. But the real
point of the poem lies in the exploitation of the incongruity of a
country boy going through a routine which belongs by convention to the city boy: the *paraklausithuron,* or nocturnal serenade
by the locked-out lover. This swain even works in learned mythological parallels in his song, in the recherché fashion of the love
elegies of the Alexandrian *literati* (and of Propertius, their Roman emulator). Ironic sport of a similar type one must constantly
be on the lookout for in Longus.

Another form of Theokritos' pastoral duplicity: VII is an apparently autobiographical account of the poet's excursion one day
out from the city to a friend's country house for a festival. On
the way they meet a "goatherd" named Lykidas and pass the
time on the road exchanging songs with him. But here is how
Lykidas introduces his song:

"This club is my gift to you," he said, "because
you're the genuine article, straight from Zeus.
But I hate the builder who tries to match Oromedon's
mountaintop with his house, and I hate those Muse-birds
who waste their time trying to outdo Homer with their croaking."
                                                    (Theokritos VII 43–49)

With these words we are drawn into a famous literary quarrel
between two of Theokritos' contemporaries as to the propriety
of attempting large-scale epic composition. It would probably
be too much to claim that Lykidas is a pastoral *persona* for Kalli-
machos (one of Theokritos' mentors), but at any rate here in
VII the pastoral is clearly an artificial setting and the pastoral
characters represent something other than they appear to be;
the pastoral has become a mask, almost *poésie à clef*. We cannot
here do justice to the full meaning of VII; Lawall has now shown
in detail how symbolically complex it actually is.[5]

In view of Theokritos' operations, one is therefore put on
guard for the original way in which Longus too will use his goatherd and shepherdess—not to mention other characters in the
story—for allusive purposes quite foreign to the normal procedures of Romance. Whether such allusiveness is chiefly or solely
to be regarded as an appropriation from the pastoral, I cannot
say, but pastoral poetry at least provides an external witness for
the plausibility of an interpretation of Longus' novel which sees
in it a symbolic texture.

After one more Idyll we must leave Theokritos. The First
Idyll is important in one way for its incorporation of the first of
Europe's surviving pastoral elegies: the lament for Daphnis (in
this case, the legendary proto-shepherd, not Longus' boy). Here
again we find a peculiar artificial, enigmatic treatment of the
figure, as if the dying Daphnis (dying from his refusal to love)
were a kind of cipher for the erotic mysteries of the poet himself.

A second importance of the poem is that in it we get to see
the Daphnis of legend, associated with gods and demigods, himself a kind of nature spirit, and mourned by representatives of
nature. It is important for us to make his acquaintance because
it is *this* Daphnis who hovers invisibly around the apparently
mundane, healthy country boy of Longus' story, as if the author
were teasingly keeping him just out of sight, an ironic double.

The final way in which the First Idyll relates to *Daphnis and
Chloe* is in its elaborate *ekphrasis* of a carved picture of an ivy-
wood bowl. This and an equally important descriptive passage
at the end of VII are representative of the kind of descriptions
of which Longus, while adding the tricks of Second Sophistic
rhetoric, provided numerous prose amplifications throughout his

book. Details from each were in fact directly plundered for use in *Daphnis and Chloe*. I quote portions of each herewith.

First Idyll:

> Inside the bowl is carved a woman—craft fit for the gods—
> dressed in gown and wimple. Two fair-haired men
> beside her, pleading their suit in turn.
> The words don't get through to her heart.
> Sometimes she smiles toward one;
> then gives her attention to the other. Their eyes
> are hollow with passion; they're wasting their time.
>
> (Theokritos I 32–38)

(In connection with the above, recall again the Dorkon-Daphnis debate, both for comparison and for contrast.)

> A little way off, a vineyard sagging with ripe grapes,
> and a little boy sitting on a fence to guard them.
> On either side, a fox. One goes along the rows,
> raiding the clusters. The other creeps up
> to the boy's lunchbag and is sure
> to keep on till she's got it.
> But he is weaving a super locust trap out of
> stalks and reeds, and is having so much fun that he
> can't be bothered with lunchbags and grapevines.
>
> (Theokritos I 45–54)

Seventh Idyll:

> Poplars and elms swayed and rustled over our heads.
> From the cave of the Nymphs nearby
> the holy water trickled and splashed.
> Russet locusts were busy babbling in the shady branches.
> From far away in the thicket came a continual murmur of the frogs.
> Larks and finches sang; the dove lamented,
> while the yellow bees bustled at the fountain.
> The smell of full-ripe summer, of harvest, was everywhere.
> Pears rolled at our feet, apples in piles beside us;
> saplings loaded with plums bent to the ground.
>
> (Theokritos VII 132–47)

Theokritos is not the whole of pastoral poetry before Longus. Apart from minor Greek successors (of whom, more later, in Chapter 7, Section II), Vergil must not be ignored. The modulations of Theokritos achieved by Vergil are enough to fill a book, and too much for here. But for the interpretation of Longus his great step was, as Bruno Snell has shown, to *invent* Arcadia; that is, invent a wholly idealized landscape.[6] Theokritos had of course not told the "whole truth" about country life, but he depicted a definite locale, whether Sicily or Kos, possessing no special mythic-romantic luster; on the contrary, definite possibilities for burlesque. Now Vergil, for reasons which the reader must seek in Snell, gave the pastoral a new, lyrically intense mythical setting in "Arcadia"—an Arcadia which was a pure poetic fiction with no factual basis in the real but quite backwoods area of the central Peloponnese which happened to provide the name.

Longus picked Lesbos, not Arcadia, as his setting. But his Lesbos has retained the mythic luster and rich connotation of Vergil's Arcadia while—and this was his special genius—continuing to afford Theokritean *bizarrerie* and comedy.

CHAPTER 5

Pastoral Infusions

IT is now time to make good the claim that the pastoral element in the composition of *Daphnis and Chloe* was the most important for the total character of the work. But in so doing, a warning should be repeated: in assessing the interaction of literary genres one must not view the process as chemical or biological. Such metaphors are at times convenient or vivid, and they are employed hereinafter. But the free initiative of the creative imagination of the author, responding to the possibilities and suggestions latent in those traditions with which he is familiar and which are related to the immediate raw material—this initiative must be kept uppermost in the conception of what goes on in the creation of the work. So in speaking of the "effect" of pastoral on *Daphnis and Chloe*, I must be taken as using a shorthand to refer to the ways in which Longus freely exploited the possibilities which surfaced in his mind at the juxtaposition of pastoral and Romance. This is not to deny that much of the end product of creation is a result of combinations unforeseen, not deliberately willed by the author; more always emerges from the great poem than the author has any notion of, and the material, though fundamentally subordinate to the creative will, does have in some ways a life of its own, as our bodies interact with our environment in ways we neither control nor observe.

Some of the points now to be made were touched on earlier. At that time they were meant to reassure the reader that the discussion actually had some relevance to *Daphnis and Chloe*. Here they are developed in a more systematic way, so that the reader may examine the ensemble of the pastoral weft, or, if you like, the whole charge of the pastoral tributaries to the narrative stream.

I *Benignity*

The most pervasive effect of pastoral is that of a universal benignification of all elements—one might best say the Arcadianizing. Extravagance, acerbity, and bombast are excluded from the style. Disorder, complex helter-skelter sensationalism, and shock are excluded from action. Villains change from Viper Fagins to Sidney Cartons. Further features of this general mollification will be pointed out repeatedly in the succeeding discussion.

II *Comedy*

Another pervasive trait, which suits and supplements the benignity, although not overtly a "pastoral" infusion, is the markedly greater introduction of themes and elements from New Comedy. Romance had always had links with drama. (One of the ancient pigeonholes for its generic classification was drama.) But in tone and allusion tragedy was the leading influence. This can be seen most clearly in Heliodoros, who takes repeated pains to underline the tragic features of his story for the reader's benefit. But Longus' pastoral benignity sorted better with New Comedy.

Apart from this basic compatibility, how is one to account for the prominence of comedy in *Daphnis and Chloe?* It *is* possible that the pastoral setting attracted comedy to it, for a number of comedies were in fact set in the country and incorporated a thematic contrast between country and city. By our good fortune, one of these was recovered, as many readers are aware, only a decade ago. This one work, all by itself, is enough to show the closeness of Longus to comedy.

Menander's Dyskolos is introduced by Pan in person, entering from one of his country shrines. He speaks, among other things, of the good will and favorable intentions which he and his neighbors, the Nymphs, hold for the country girl next door, who, like Daphnis and Chloe, is instant in her devotion to these rural gods. By divine influence, including those prophetic-instructive dreams which come so readily in *Daphnis and Chloe* too, the maid is happily married off at the end to a city-style boy much like Astylos (whose name means just that) in his soft and feckless

good nature. The final family party at the shrine in the country
shows how much the festivities at the ends of Books II and IV
in Longus probably owe to similar scenes in New Comedy. Furthermore, the city boy has a parasite who, given the proper circumstances (i.e., a different play) could easily turn up as Astylos'
Gnathon. (Gnathon is a standard name in New Comedy for a
parasite; not surprisingly, since it means jaw-man.) The *Dyskolos*
gives us also an instance of another comic perennial: the good
and faithful servant who helps prevent trouble; in Longus, it is
Astylos' servant Eudromos ("Good-runner") who is instrumental
to Daphnis' eventual happiness.

Features of *Daphnis and Chloe* which are missing in the
Dyskolos, but which infallibly derive from comedy include: (1)
The party girl or hetaira, who—especially in Menander—is often
a kind of heroine. Lykainion on several grounds is clearly an
adaptation of this type. Her name means "Little Wolf"; wolf
was slang for prostitute; the diminutive suffix is frequent in the
names of professional sweethearts. As often in comedy, she helps
a boy-girl pair out of difficulties. (2) Daphnis' peasant rivals for
the hand of Chloe are also the property of comedy where love
often wins out against the threat of a wedding contracted elsewhere. (3) The exposure of children and their eventual restoration thanks to birth tokens are recurrent comic themes.

In one quaint moment Longus seems actually to be comedizing
for the sheer fun of it: the exigencies of staging forbade indoor
episodes, so for many consultations the comic author was obliged
to make his characters enter artificially from indoors onto the
street (i.e., the stage); then after the confabulation they would
make an equally unmotivated exit. No such restraint was placed
on Longus, obviously, yet when Lamon hears of Gnathon's plan
to get possession of Daphnis, he calls Myrtale out of doors, tells
her it is time to reveal the birth tokens; then they both go back
inside.

Despite the magnetic attraction which the pastoral style doubtless exercised on comedy, another strong reason for the presence
of comic motifs in Longus is derived from the literary fashion
of his day: The Atticist revival had restored New Comedy, as
one of the founts of Attic pure and undefiled, to a position of
high esteem among aspirant Atticists. One most striking body of
evidence for this is the art-letters of Alkiphron and Aelian, which

are filled with curious thefts from comedy—several directly from the *Dyskolos*, as can now be seen.

In this connection a special problem of interpretation exists. Some of Alkiphron's "thefts" seem to be directly from Longus. Yet much learned argumentation has left the question still open: perhaps the theft was the other way round; perhaps both drew on a third source, which may even have been comedy.[1] At any rate, as a sample of the way in which author fed on author in this period, compare the following with Longus' description of Daphnis' winter fowling:

Vintner to Workwell: This year the winter is very bad, and no one can get out of doors. For the snow has covered everything, and it's not just the hills are blossoming white, but the low places too. Hard to find anything to do; but sitting around idle is a disgrace. So I peek out of the hut, and as soon as I crack the door I see a whole mob of birds coming along with the snow—blackbirds and thrushes. So right away I get some birdlime out of the pot and smear it on the pear-branches. The swarm of birds has hardly settled down before they are all hanging there from the branches, caught fast by their wings or heads or feet—quite a sight. (Alkiphron II 27, Benner and Fobes)

III *Style*

On the simplest level the effect of pastorality can be seen in that special rhetorical character of Longus which was pointed out in Chapter 3. It consists first of all in the remarkable transparency and simplicity of his language, especially in narrative passages. Ancient arbiters of style regarded pastoral subject matter as suited to "sweetness" (*glykytes:* Hermogenes) or the "smooth" (*glaphyros:* Demetrios) style—characteristics strongly marked in Longus.[2] I find Oscar Wilde's *Fairy Stories* an intriguing parallel to meditate on for catching the special flavor of Longus: here too a supersophisticated, overripe stylist deliberately adopts an almost cloying simplicity and prettiness to fit his subject:

In every tree that he could see there was a little child. And the trees were so glad to have the children back again that they had covered themselves with blossoms, and were waving their arms gently above the children's heads. The birds were flying about and twittering with delight, and the flowers were looking up through the green grass and laughing.[3]

The comparison, of course, ignores the archness of Longus, and his indulgence in all the Asianic word music. Wilde makes some approaches to this in the *Fairy Stories*, but he does not pull out all the stops.[4] For this one must turn back to John Lyly, who sprinkles rhyme, alliteration, and assonance generously upon his parallel or antithetical groups of clauses:

Doe we not commonly see that in paynted pottes is hidde the dead-lyest poyson? that in the greenest grasse is the greatest serpent? . . . How franticke are those lovers which are carryed away with the gaye glistering of the fine face? the beautie whereof is parched with the Sommers blase, & chipped with the winters blast, which is of so short continuance that it fadeth before one perceive it florishe, of so small profit that it poysoneth those that possess, of so little value with the wyse, that they accompt it a delicate bayte with a deadly hooke, a sweete *Panther* with a devouring paunch, a sower poyson in a silver potte.[5]

Despite Longus' Asianism, if the reader will but recall what wondrous oddities of baroque complexity the Asianic wave was capable of inducing in other Romances (Achilleus Tatios, Heliodoros), the influence of the pastoral in the relative simplicity and discretion of Longus will be sufficiently manifest. Among the best assessments of that style is that of the eighteenth-century French scholar d'Ansse de Villoison, who deserves to be quoted:

The diction of Longus is pure, bright, and agreeable: broken into short phrases, yet still rhythmic, without lurching; sweeter than honey, it flows like a silver stream shaded on each side by trees, and so blossomy, decorated, and finished that all the elegance of word and thought could be gathered from it. . . . [Apart from some inappropriateness of subject] I know of no writer whom beginners in Greek, needing some enticement, should come to earlier, for the astonishing fluency, aptness, elegance, agreeableness, sportiveness, and amplitude of his language. This is not to deny that sometimes even he departs from the old simple, unaffected freshness and indulges in the wayward luxuries of the later sophists, putting curling irons to his prose, using far-fetched expressions, letting his wit get the better of him.[6]

This is the point for a weighty digression: in the light of such a style, what are we to say about the various translations available? There is currently much debate on the right way to translate.[7] My own position must be stated: that version is generally preferable—no matter how "free"— which catches fire from the original, even if (to adapt Hopkins) it only "admires and does otherwise." [8] Such a translation will of course often be useless for purposes of scholarly study of a work and its position in the history of literature, but literature is not *Wissenschaft*. Two translations of this sort I am acquainted with: those of Amyot and Thornley. (Those by Angel Day and George Moore are worthy runners-up.)

The value of quotation in a matter like this depends on the fairness of the choice: is it a representative passage? I think I am being fair when I ask the reader to compare Thornley's free fire with Moses Hadas' sluggish rendering of the following:

Hadas:
When they heard the caroling of the birds they too burst into song; when they saw the sportive lambs they too skipped lightly about; and the bees they imitated by gathering flowers. . . . Their amusements were of a childish and pastoral kind. Chloe would go hunting asphodel stalks, of which she wove traps for grasshoppers, neglecting her flock the while. Daphnis cut slender reeds, perforated the intervals between the joints, fitted them together with soft wax, and then practiced piping till nightfall.[9]

Thornley:
Hearing how the birds did chant it, they began to carol too, and seeing how the lambs skipt, tript their light and nimble measures. Then, to emulate the bees, they fall to cull the fairest flowers. . . . For all their sports were sports of children and of shepherds. Chloe, scudding up and down and here and there picking up the windlestraws, would make in plats a cage for a grasshopper, and be so wholly bent on that, that she was careless of her flocks. Daphnis on the other side, having cut the slender reeds and bored the quills or intervals between the joints, and with his soft wax joined and fitted one to another, took no care but to practice or devise some tune even from morning to the twilight.[10]

Hadas faithfully labors along, giving us more or less a straight translation. But English is not light enough—or its denotative equivalents to Longus' text will not trip along lightly enough, anyway—so the effect is stodgy: Mozart orchestrated by Max

Reger. (Something similar can be said for two currently famous
"faithful" efforts by excellent men of letters: Lattimore's *Iliad*
and C. Day Lewis' *Aeneid.*)

Knowingly or not, Thornley has solved the difficulty of *Daphnis
and Chloe* in English. To match the direct simplicity of Longus'
diction in English would have been pallid, as Hadas is pallid.
This the Greek is not, because of the purely musical features of
the Greek language in general and the particular combinations
thereof which Longus here achieves. It would be possible, with
considerable labor, to create an English text which would match
the Greek in its limpid light syllabic melody, but this would require a most exhaustive search and selection of the right English
words, and these words would force the translator to make radical departures from the detail of the description—and even of
the narrative—in the original.

Thornley hits upon the solution: create a text which has some
equivalent interest on the verbal level, without dislocating the
description and narrative. Thornley's equivalent interest lies in
the quite un-Longian choice of quaint, out-of-the-way, rustic, or
old-fashioned words, and paraphrase. All sorts of possibilities
exist in modern English for an approach comparable to Thornley's: perhaps the use of some current slang, or camp, or ethnic
idiom. Once more: this would not be the Longus of Greek literature; it would, however, be some genuine sort of English Longus.
The assignment remains open—to some willful linguistic pres-
tidigitator like Nabokov, Updike, or Barth.

The only current readable version is that of Paul Turner:

Hearing the birds singing they burst into song, seeing the lambs gam-
bolling they danced nimbly about, and taking their cue from the bees
they started gathering flowers. . . . Their toys were of a pastoral and
childish nature. . . . Chloe would go off somewhere and pick up
some stalks of corn which she would weave into a cage for a locust;
and while she was working on it she would forget about the sheep.
And Daphnis, after cutting some slender reeds, piercing them at the
joints, and fastening them together with soft wax, would practice
playing the Pan-pipe until it was dark.[11]

But, as is clear from this example, Turner, in quest for a smooth
reading, has lost the verve. Everything shaggy or wayward is
carefully sanded off. It is a *koinê Daphnis and Chloe* for news-

paper readers. There is, however, none for the twentieth-century reader of literature in English, so far as I can see.[12]

IV *Antiphon*

The narrative of any Romance, since it involves two main characters who spend a good deal of the time in separation, is likely to oscillate between the two, producing a certain degree of parallelism as the plot advances. But such parallelism is present to a far greater degree in Daphnis and Chloe, and that without the vast separations which occur in the other novels. To begin with, consider the basic alignment:

Pan – Nymphs
Daphnis – Chloe
Goats – Sheep
Lamon – Myrtale
Dryas – Nape

Pan and the Nymphs are, of course, the consequence of a country setting (compare Menander's *Dyskolos*). But, to my knowledge, Longus is the only author to bring them into paired association with the hero and heroine of a Romantic narrative (or drama). Again, it is standard in Theokritos to pair shepherd against goatherd, but Longus was the first to exploit the symmetry in a full narrative, with the goats going naturally to the side of Pan (the goat-foot horned god) and the male.

Now consider the following scheme:[13]

Daphnis found	Chloe found
Chloe struck by Daphnis' beauty	Daphnis struck by Chloe's beauty
Dorkon tries to rape Chloe; she is saved	Pirates kidnap Daphnis; he is saved
Daphnis attacked by Methymnaean youths, saved	Chloe abducted by Methymnaean fleet; saved
Daphnis instructed by amorous Lykainion	Chloe besieged by suitors
Sequence leading to Daphnis' recognition	Sequence leading to Chloe's recognition

From this it should be clear that the amoebeic or antiphonal principle of arrangement which is strongly associated with pas-

toral poetry shows itself not only in those explicit imitations of
pastoral amoebeism, such as the debate between Dorkon and
Daphnis, but also in the architecture of the work as a whole.
Only two other major works in antiquity, so far as I know, can
lay claim to such an architectonic application of the amoebeic
principle: Vergil's *Georgics* and *Aeneid*. (And the amoebeism of
these latter works is by no means agreed upon, a discussion I
will not here enter into.)[14]

V *Plausibility*

One quite radical contribution of pastoral to the Romance is
that it renders the locale for the action essentially single. So
long as Daphnis and Chloe are to be goatherd and shepherdess,
their tie to the pasturing fields will keep them in one spot. The
irruptions of fortune are there, but they do no more than take
Daphnis a little way off shore, and Chloe a few miles down the
coast, whereas the standard Romance battens on the most improbably transcontinental relocations. Longus, as part of the pastoral benignity of his plan, retains mere hints of these geographi-
cal vicissitudes, mere playful remnants with all the sober sensationalism and melodrama leached out. It is as if he were giving an
ironic bow to the tradition, and then going ahead to use the
material for his own quite different purposes.

The effect on the plot is thus to bestow a greater degree of
plausibility in the sequence of the action. In fact, Longus' markedly increased attention to the coherence of his plot has been
widely noted. The closer connection which he established with
New Comedy doubtless contributed to this coherence, for a notable feature of New Comedy is the skill with which it preserves
the causal interconnections of an often rather intricate plot.

Two special examples are frequently cited. The first, in Book I,
is the continuous sequence beginning with the wolf's incursions
and ending with Chloe beauty-struck by Daphnis. The second
instance, in Book II, is another case of what must be Longus'
sheer playfulness—here shown in the elaborate triviality of the
initial causes: it begins with the pleasure cruise of the Methymnaean playboys and ends with Chloe's abduction. First, the hawser is stolen and replaced by a wicker rope; then Daphnis' goats
are frightened down from the hills to the shore by the hounds
of the playboy hunting party; in quest for forage along the sand,

one goat eats the rope; the ship is carried out to sea; the youths seize Daphnis in revenge; Daphnis is set free and the youths are chased off; their complaint raises the naval expedition; the raiders carry off Chloe. And at this point the action continues through direct divine intervention, which according to conventional canons of plot criticism would have to be relegated to the *ex machina*, or implausible, category.

About this divine intervention there will be more to say later, in Chapter 6; for the present, two remarks: It is curious that, side by side with its maximum plausibility, Longus' novel introduces more, and more direct, ingressions of the supernatural into the action than do the other Romances. At the same time—and this too will be shown in Chapter 6—these ingressions are, through Longus' art and intent, much more profoundly natural (and therefore plausible at a deep level) than all the outrageous mechanical coincidences of the other Romances.

VI *Functional Digressions*

As earlier noted, like the other two Romances with high literary pretensions along Second Sophistic lines, *Daphnis and Chloe* has its encyclopedic digressions. Now in Achilleus Tatios one finds such things as the origin of purple dye (II 11), or the pan-pipes (VIII 6), or the story of the nightingale (V 5). But in each case these accounts stop the main narrative in its tracks, for the enjoyment of gratuitous irrelevance. For Longus, by contrast, Schönberger and Chalk have in different ways pointed out how the three digressive stories subtly correspond to the point which the main action has reached.[15] This correspondence is assisted by the fact that the digressions are themselves pastoralized.

In Book I Daphnis tells Chloe the following: The mourning dove (*Phassa*, in Greek) had once been a maid so musical she could govern her herd of cattle by song and pipe alone. A youth nearby, however, managed to excel her in skill and drew away thereby her eight best cows to his own herd. The girl in her vexation begged the gods to change her to a bird, and they did. She still mourns (I 27).

Now all three stories are etiological metamorphoses; all involve music, whether human, divine, or natural. Further, all contrast with the main narrative by ending unhappily, each time with an increasing element of active violence. But at the same

time there are specific parallels. Here in the Phassa story the girl
and boy are neighboring herdsmen; musical control of flocks has
already been hinted at in I 13, and will be thematic throughout
the Romance; Eros is still unknown to Daphnis and Chloe, so in
the case of Phassa there is no erotic element (whereas it is present in both subsequent stories, and is common in such tales generally); the unnamed boy surpasses Phassa in musicianship:
Daphnis is Chloe's musical instructor; Chloe crowns her head
with pine twigs, like Phassa.

The second story—of Pan's erotic chase after Syrinx—comes in
II 34 after the rescue of Chloe by Pan from the Methymnaean
fleet, a rescue in which the music of the pan-pipes (*syrinx* in
Greek) was a prominent factor. The story is told while the company is waiting for Philetas' great *syrinx* to be fetched from home.
Later in the party Daphnis and Chloe, who are now explicitly
in love, give a mimic dance of the story.

Daphnis tells Chloe about Echo in III 23, just after he has had
his erotic lesson from Lykainion and has decided to forgo his own
pleasure out of consideration for Chloe's virginity. In the story,
on the other hand, Echo, whose virginal vocation is brought out
(in contrast to Phassa and Syrinx), is torn apart at vengeful Pan's
instigation. This dismemberment (*sparagmos*), through its association with Orpheus and Dionysos, connotes the other side of
Eros-Dionysos: destructive violence, a foreshadowing of Lampis'
ravage of the garden, and of the violent scenes depicted in the
Dionysos shrine in that garden.[16] Here, however, the violence
pointedly contrasts with Daphnis' unwillingness to hurt Chloe.

VII *Paramelodrama*

Along with plausibility and functionality, his pastoral benignity
leads Longus to purge all earnest quest for shock and sensation.
Contrast the following with Longus:

> Then at a signal everyone drew back from the altar. One of the
> two young men stretched her out flat on her back and bound her to
> pegs fastened in the earth, as sculptors show Marsyas bound to the
> tree. Then he took a sword, plunged it into her heart; dragging it
> down through her abdomen, he sliced her open. Her intestines surged
> right forth, and they pulled them away with their hands and laid them
> on the altar. After they were roasted, they all cut them into servings
> and ate.

Watching all this, the soldiers and the general cried out at each new act and turned their faces away from the sight. I, under the influence of the utter strangeness of it, sat and gazed like a spectator. But it was a kind of paralysis: for the outrage, in its measurelessness, had crazed me like a thunderbolt. (Achilleus Tatios III 15)

A passage like this is best savored by the modern reader under the aegis of literary Pop Art; in fact, much of ancient Romance is rich with the opulence of Camp. And Longus' treatment of such material shows a sensibility which is analogous to a modern taste for Camp: he short-circuits the vulgar electricity; soaks out the poison with a pastoral poultice. In the same way, some dreadful frame from our tragic-strips acquires geniality when rooted out from the sinister luxuriance of its patch on the back pages and pegged to a gallery wall.

The muted treatment of sensational material is part of Longus' general fastidious trifling with the Romance tradition. Compare the curiously sober learned footnotes in Achilleus Tatios on the zoology of the elephant or crocodile with Longus' afterword to the swimming escape which the cattle make from the pirates:

As a matter of fact, your cow swims better than a man; it is surpassed only by waterfowl and the fish themselves. Nor would a cow ever drown while swimming, unless its hooves should fall off, once they get soaked through. (I 30)

To return to the disembowellment scene in Achilleus Tatios: the nearest Longus ever comes to such *al dente* tripe is in the reference to the dismemberment of Echo, or in the symbolic *sparagmos* which befalls Dionysophanes' garden. Other violence and cruelty is similarly muted.

Likewise, the traditional villains of Romance are here given softhearted stand-ins. Dorkon's misdemeanors are counterbalanced by the comically humiliating failure of his attempted wolf-rape, and by his love-in-death recantation. Lykainion supplies the traditional Potiphar's Wife role, but what an unselfish, helpful, provident version! (This modulation occurs partly because she is conceived in terms of the goodhearted courtesan of New Comedy; as earlier stated, her name, in both root and suffix, supports the connection.) The repulsive Gnathon is meant to ingratiate after all with his fervid sophistic lover's eloquence (IV 17), and he makes amends to Daphnis by rescuing Chloe from Lampis. Even this last villain is forgiven and is last seen helping out with the wedding music.

Similarly with the "pocket war" between Mitylene and Methymna. In Chariton, Heliodoros, and Achilleus Tatios, whole armies and navies are destroyed, in battles whose descriptions consciously emulate the classic pages in Herodotus, Thucydides, and Xenophon. But at the beginning of Book III of *Daphnis and Chloe*, the Mitylenean expedition gets no taste of hostilities at all; the affair is closed off with negotiations. Why does Longus put in this apparently pointless episode? The answer clearly is that it is one more deliberate pastoral defusing of the old Romantic bombs.

VIII *Simplicity*

Longus' story is bound to a natural setting. A concomitant of this is that Longus ties his action to the rhythm of the seasons. The other Romances pay little if any attention to the time of year; they certainly do not let the season color the nature of an entire sequence of events, as Longus does. (There is a further significance to this seasonal rhythm which will be taken up in Chapter 6. At this point it is the effect on the arrangement of the plot that is the issue.)

Even in the relatively simple plot of Chariton, the action is jerked backward and forward by a number of breathtaking "meanwhiles" as we pass from one of the pair to the other. The dislocation of the temporal sequence of the narrative is boldly laid hold of by Heliodoros and exaggerated to a degree unparalleled in any other ancient narrative: in an obvious outbidding of the *Odyssey* he inserts not just one flashback narrative, but a second inside the first. Furthermore, the exposition is artificially delayed, so that the information necessary for the understanding of the opening scene is not provided until halfway through the novel. Achilleus Tatios does not equal this superb mannerism, but is nevertheless quite sufficiently baroque.

But for Longus the linear progression of the seasons fixes the movement of the action. With the exception of the secret of the birth of Daphnis and Chloe, we begin at the beginning and move steadily along from event to event until the end. Once more, the effect of pastoral has been to dissolve the harshness and extravagance of the Romance tradition in plot construction.

Furthermore, the movement of the year supports and parallels the phases of the growing passion of Daphnis and Chloe: spring begins it, summer heightens it, the fall bears fruit in the revelation of Eros. Winter is the dead season through which their love struggles as best it can. The next spring is love's rebirth, bringing new carnal knowledge to Daphnis. Summer tests his self-control; fall brings the final fruit, marriage.

One very particular bonus comes to the story from its involvement with the seasonal movement. Instead of Romance's usual tedious display of overwhelming love-at-first-sight, the love of Daphnis and Chloe is a natural growth, like the year and their own maturation. Its approach is imperceptible until, at a certain moment (the bath of Daphnis), one notices it is there.

IX *Pastoral Sport*

There are a number of miscellaneous consequences of the pastoral. I shall jumble them out here before passing on to the final section. They all relate to the tone of playful, ironic condescension, the loss of overt seriousness which comes from the distancing of subject via pastorality.

First, there is what one might call innocent lubricity: all the straight-faced teasing which so aroused the moral disapprobation of serious romantics and others. At its mildest: Daphnis is hauled out of the wolf trap by Chloe's breast-band. More prurient: at the bath, Chloe's fingers sink luxuriously into Daphnis' flesh. When Chloe sleeps, a cicada flies for refuge into her bosom; Daphnis reaches in to catch it. And there are some naïve experiments at a cure for their love fever, climaxed with the titillating scene of Daphnis' initiation by Lykainion. For such passages the pseudo-Theokritean Idyll No. 27 in which a cowherd named Daphnis makes love to a goatgirl, may have served as a crude antecedent. (But is all the teasing just that? Part of the fascination, the perennial vitality, of Longus lies in the fact that one can answer both yes and no. For the no side of the answer, see the discussion in Chapter 6 of the symbolic context in which these apparently lubricious and false-naïve passages are set.)

Just as pastoral is used to produce a comic-grotesque rustic

version of the urban *paraklausithuron* in Theokritos' *Third Idyll,*
so Longus seems to aim at the pleasantly absurd and incongruous:
in the rescue of Daphnis from the pirates, the boat is swamped
because the cattle jump off all together from one side. His learned
footnote on the swimming abilities of oxen, and the coming-out
and going-in of Dryas and Nape as if on stage, are similar instances.

Longus is fond of a pastoral version of Pope's "art of sinking,"
or bathos, where at the supposed culmination of a passage one
is dropped flat with a lapse into rusticity. In Theokritos III the
hopeless swain threatens suicide: "I'll take off my jacket and jump
into the water/—right there where fisherman Olpis keeps a lookout for tunnies!" (III 25–26). And after he has finished his proud
parade of mythological lore: "I have a headache, but that doesn't
mean anything to you!" (III 52). Similarly, Longus blunts cli-
maxes by agrarian deflection:

[Chloe's amorous distress:] Now she would laugh, now weep; at one
moment she was sleeping, at the next she jumped out of bed; her face
was pale, and then again it flamed with blushes. Not even a cow stung
by a gadfly puts on such a show. (I 13)

[Philetas' discourse on Eros:] He rules the elements and rules the
stars; he rules the gods who are his peers; not even you are such rulers
over your goats and sheep. . . . For him the rivers flow and the
winds blow. I have even known a bull to be enamored, and he roared
as if stung by a gadfly; and I have known a buck to fall in love with
a goat, and he followed her everywhere. (II 7)

Related to pastoral bathos is the transparently artificial naïveté
which Longus bestows on Daphnis and Chloe. When they hear
Philetas' advice, their reaction is:

We must try out all the cures he spoke of: kissing and embracing and
lying naked on the ground. It is cold, but if Philetas could do it, we'll
go through with it too. (II 9)

A person who can savor the artifice of the following passage is
well on the way to full enjoyment of Longus. This is the winter
dialogue of Daphnis and Chloe out in the snow; it is their first
chance to talk in private during Daphnis' visit to Chloe's home:

"I came because of you, Chloe."

"I know, Daphnis."

"It's because of you I am killing these poor birds."

"What do you want me to do, Daphnis?"

"Remember me."

"I do remember you, I swear by the Nymphs, who witnessed my oath back then in that cave; we'll go there again when the snow melts."

"But there's so much snow, Chloe, and I'm afraid I'll melt before it does."

"Cheer up, Daphnis, the sun is hot."

"I hope it gets as hot as the fire in my heart, Chloe."

"You're just kidding me."

"By the goats, I swear I'm not—those goats you made me swear by." (III 10)

The keynotes of the passage are: the shy, gulping brevity of the two opening phrases (six words, not nine, in the Greek); "remember me"; the outworn urban love tropes of melting and burning in a rustic's mouth (and here neatly fitted to the winter meeting); Chloe's "you're kidding," and Daphnis' incongruous "by the goats!"

One last example:

[As soon as Daphnis has learned his lesson from Lykainion:] Daphnis, still with a rustic's mentality, was eager to run to Chloe and try out everything he had learned, as if afraid he would forget if he waited around. (III 19)

X Flosculi

An association with pastoral makes it almost inevitable that not only individual words and phrases from the pastoral poets will be intessellated in the text, but also whole passages will be picked up by Longus and reworked into an allusive paraphrase of the original, like little flowers (*flosculi*) worked into a pattern. Theokritos of course is the chief contributor here, but the other poets traditionally called bucolic (Bion and Moschos) make their appearance as well. Since the pastoral involves not only the country, but love also, there was every reason for Longus not to stop there, but to go on to include honorific thefts from Greek love lyric at large. All Romance prose likes to rifle poetry, but Longus does it superabundantly. As Valley says:

Longus is an eclectic. Like an industrious bee he gathers his honey
from the works of the older poets and *prosateurs*. With a sophistic
artistry probably never surpassed, he integrates all this diversity. Careful judgment and good taste aid him in the attainment of unity; his
mastery of his material is exemplary. . . . With the exception of
Vergil (in the *Eclogues*) and the Byzantine Niketas Eugenianus there
can hardly be another Greek or Latin author who has plundered
Theokritos' *Idylls* to the extent that Longus has. One is inclined to
assert that, in their absence, the depiction of Daphnis and Chloe
would never have seen the light of day.[17]

One really ought not, however, employ the metaphor of thievery
with Longus, for he makes the passages his own, giving them a
specific and characteristic twist which fixes them firmly in their
new contexts. Take for example the passage at the end of Theokritos VII, which was quoted in Chapter 4. Longus interweaves
it into his description of the first high summer of his story. I shall
italicize the words and phrases which, taken in their ensemble,
betray the reminiscence of Theokritos VII:

Spring was now at an end and *summer* was under way, and *everything was at its peak:* trees filled with fruit, fields filled with grain;
the cicadas were pleasantly cheeping, fruit-perfume blew sweetly,
the sheep joyfully bleated. One would have supposed the *rivers to be
singing* in their quiet flowing, the winds to be piping in the pines with
their blowing; that when *the apples fell to the ground,* it was for love;
that the sun stripped everyone out of fondness for beauty (I 23)

In addition to the Seventh Idyll, the opening of the First Idyll
has also been blended in:

> The pine by the springs rustles a sweet melody,
> friend goatman, and the pipes you play
> are just as sweet. First prize comes to Pan;
>   but you are next.
>   (Theokritos I 1–3)

The characteristic transformation Longus works upon his poets
is twofold. First of course comes the rephrasing and restructuring
in terms of his own rhetorical preciosity: in the passage above,
for instance, the grouping of short phrases in pairs or triads, often
rhyming—as the translation is meant to imitate. But there is

further the pushing of descriptive metaphor into conceit; that is, to a point where the suggestiveness of the description is not the chief literary aim, but must share the attention with the interest of literary concoction for its own sake. In Theokritos I, the pine makes melody; in Longus, the rivers *sing* (a more personifying word in the Greek), and the winds literally *play the pan-pipes*. In Theokritos VII, the apples roll on the ground; in Longus, they fall *amorously*. There is in addition here a play on the Greek custom of the thrown apple as a love-token.[18]

This quest for point and wit (analogous to his puns and other word play) perhaps betrays Longus' attachment to the tradition of the Greek epigram, particularly the love epigrams of Meleagros. Here is a brief sample of the way in which Meleagros turns description into conceit:

> The eyes of Asclepias are like the ocean in
> a bright blue smiling mood:
> "Come along out for a sail on me!"
> (*Greek Anthology* V 156)

In fact, a number of passages in Longus are clear implantations from the epigrammatists; the special piquancy of his treatment of them derives from the fact that they are given a pastoral modulation. Some examples: an old formula of love poetry takes the form "I wish I were X so that she would be Y," as in:

> I wish I were the wind, and you, walking on the shore,
> would bare your breasts and take me wafted to you.
> (*Greek Anthology* V 83)

This formula is used in three places by Longus, as for example in "I wish I were his pan-flute, so he might breathe into me; I wish I were a goat, so he could graze me" (I 14). (The Greek for "graze" has an additional nuance of "handle" as well.)

The topos of lover drinking out of the cup after his beloved (preserved for English in Ben Jonson's "To Celia") is used twice by Longus. Once, more or less conventionally (III 8), but once clearly in a rustic re-formation:

He would also teach her to play the pan-pipes, and when she had started to blow he would snatch the pipes and run over the reeds with his own lips: thus he made a show of correcting her mistakes, but through this pretext he would manage to kiss Chloe via the pipes. (I 24)

The poet most in evidence after Theokritos is, like Theokritos, especially apt to Longus' subject. Sappho for the Greeks was one of the greatest, if not the greatest, of the love poets, and her native island, Lesbos, thanks to her and her compatriot Alkaios, came to be regarded as the place of lyric passion par excellence. Among the speculations as to why Longus locates his story on Lesbos instead of the traditionally pastoral Sicily, Kos, or Arcadia, is the claim that the erotic aura bestowed upon it by Sappho's reputation drew him to this setting. (Other speculations are that Lesbos was Longus' own home; or that the island had a religious connection with the story—on which, more in Chapter 6.)

One of Sappho's legacies to Greek Romance was her archetypal description of the psychosomatic symptoms of an erotic on-slaught, in the famous *phainetai moi kenos:*

That man seems equal to gods, who sits before you,
and hears close up your sweet-talk,
your sweet laughter, which rattles my heart in my rib-cage.
Because, when I look at you, my voice doesn't come any more,
my tongue collapses, thin fire runs along under my skin;
no sight in my eyes, my ears are roaring,
sweat pours over me, I tremble all over, paler than
grass, only a little way off from death.

(No. 31, Lobel and Page)

The description of such erotic ravages became a much-trodden topos, inherited by Longus along with the rest of the Romantic equipment. But Longus, alone among Romancers so far as I know, brings the wheel full circle with explicit acknowledgment of his debt to the foundress in the last clause of the following:

He would often get the chills, and he pressed on his throbbing heart; and he would wish to look at Chloe, but when looking he would be covered with blushes; [thus far, more or less standard stuff—and he wouldn't eat or drink or talk or frisk about, *and*] his face was paler than grass in the summer. (I 17)

There are several more extensive and characteristically transformed adaptations from Sappho. At the end of Book III, when
Daphnis, so far as in him lies, has completed the negotiations to
marry Chloe and has been hailed as "Chloe's husband" by Dryas,
the following episode brings the book to a close:

> [Daphnis and Chloe have gone to the fields:] They went around look-
> ing for ripe fruit. Of this there was plenty, for it was the prime season:
> many pears both wild and orchard, many apples, some already fallen
> to the ground, some still on the branches. Those on the ground were
> more fragrant, but those on the branches more colorful. The ones gave
> off the breath of wine, the others gleamed like gold. One apple tree
> had been picked; no fruit or leaf remained; all branches were bare—
> but one apple waved at the top, on the highest branch. It was large
> and fair, and by itself outperfumed the crowd of fruit elsewhere. The
> apple-picker had been afraid to climb that high, had let it go. And
> perhaps the fair fruit was being kept for an Erotic shepherd. (III 33)

(Note in passing that here again Longus is reminiscing on Theokritos VII.) Daphnis wants to climb up and get the apple. Chloe
tries to stop him; he goes ahead while Chloe marches off in a
huff; he gets it and presents it to her as a beauty prize in imitation of the way Paris, while he was shepherd on Mount Ida,
awarded the golden apple as beauty prize to Aphrodite. So
Chloe is for a moment the queen and goddess of love. But why
all this about the last apple left at the top? Sappho:

> . . . as the sweet-apple reddens on the branch at the top,
> high on the highest branch; and the apple-pickers didn't
> see it—no, they saw it, but couldn't reach it . . .
> (No. 105a, Lobel and Page)

This is a fragment from one of Sappho's wedding songs, and this
symbolism of the apple becomes clear once this context is recognized. But the plucking of the apple—in Longus at least—does
not represent just the winning of the bride. Chloe tries to stop
Daphnis and becomes vexed when he persists. So here, at the
point where the marriage of Daphnis and Chloe—save for the
sanction of their master—is assured, we have a gentle symbolic
foreshadowing of the consummation of that marriage, including

even the virgin's conventional reluctance. (In one of Sappho's
wedding-song fragments the bride cries out, "Maidenhood, my
maidenhood, where are you going, now that you leave me?" and
Maidenhood replies, "I shall never come back to you" [No. 114
Lobel and Page].)

This instance of the way Longus allusively employs his source
to suggest a significance beyond the literal may serve as a preparation for the full diapason of his symbolic resources which we
shall soon be discussing in Chapter 6. And we have still not
exhausted the resonances of this passage. For, as Daphnis hands
the fruit to Chloe, he says, to justify his refusal to acquiesce in
her reluctance:

Maiden, the lovely Seasons made this apple grow, and a lovely tree
nurtured it while the sun was ripening it, and Fortune preserved it.
So long as I had eyes to see, I wasn't going to let it go—it would have
fallen and been trampled by a grazing sheep or polluted by a sliding
snake or consumed by time as it lay there; yet there I was seeing it
and praising. This was Aphrodite's beauty prize; take this as your
victory gift from me. (III 34)

Perhaps it will not rub off all the bloom to say that this is a
subtle, profoundly healthy version of the old *carpe diem*, one
almost worthy to be used to countervail Hopkins' celebration of
abstinence in "The Leaden Echo and the Golden Echo":

Come then, your ways and airs and looks, locks, maiden
gear, gallantry and gaiety and grace,
Winning ways, airs innocent, maiden manners, sweet looks,
loose locks, long locks, lovelocks, gaygear, going
gallant, girlgrace—
Resign them, sign them, seal them, send them, motion them
with breath,
And with sighs soaring, soaring sighs deliver
them; beauty-in-the-ghost, deliver it, early now, long
before death
Give beauty back, beauty; beauty, beauty, back to God,
beauty's self and beauty's giver.

The intent of the passage in Longus, and its freshness, will come
out most clearly if put beside a traditional form of the *carpe diem:*

> Hoarding your maidenhood! And what will you
> get out of that? When you get to Hades,
> girl, there will be no lover.
> The pleasures of Kypris are for the living;
> down *there,* we shall lie down—all bones and dust.
> (Asclepiades, *Greek Anthology* V 85)

Longus also uses Sappho in a passage which hints at even wider significance, the description of the garden trampled and torn by Lampis:

Even a stranger coming up would have wept. For the place had been defiled, and the ground was like a bog. But some flowers that had escaped the outrage still gleamed through and kept their beauty, even there in the mud. And the bees kept on crowding around them, incessantly buzzing like mourners. (IV 8)

Compare Sappho's fragment:

> . . . as shepherds in the hills trample the hyacinth
> under foot
> and the dark red blossom lies there on the ground.
> (No. 105c, Lobel and Page)

This fragment is often interpreted as referring either to the bride's loss of virginity or to the unwed maid's loss of chastity. It clearly is involved in Daphnis' *apologia* for apple-picking quoted above. But here in the defiled garden, with the help of a symbolism later to be spelled out more fully, Longus uses it to suggest a universal erotic destructiveness and violence, which will have its place in a fundamentally religious economy of life involving rebirth and new growth after loss.[19] (In our present passage the bees, even though they are compared with mourners, may, through associations given them in the ancient world, hint at this regeneration.) [20]

Once more: this inundation and fecundation of Longus' tale by lyric poetry is chiefly enabled and organized by his pastorality. Second Sophistic orators and their Romantic followers loved to plunder from lyric and use its blossoms for special florid pages; pastoral gave Longus a right of anthology ("flower-gathering") denied to all others. In exercising that right, he did not simply collect and arrange. Through pastoral baptism all was changed. Longus was, as it were, the enraptured rusticate of Marvell's "The Garden,"

> Annihilating all that's made
> To a green thought in a green shade.

CHAPTER 6

Hybrid Virtues I: Divine Immanence

> Nature is a temple where living pillars
> sometimes effuse intricate utterance;
> man moves through it past forests of symbols
> which gaze at him with familiar eyes.
>
> (Baudelaire, "Correspondences")

> The wisdom . . . by which the cosmos is ruled even down to the
> leaves flying in the wind.
>
> (St. Augustine, *Confessions* VII 6)

HITHERTO we have been considering the unilateral contribution of pastoral to Longus' Romance. But several most important aspects of *Daphnis and Chloe* result from reciprocal interaction between the possibilities of pastoral and those of Romance. To take in this panorama we must begin by stepping rather far back.

Greek Romances in general have one utterly basic defect, which one might call "the flight from the real." If the Romance material had the intrinsic interest of a dream-vision, where, however unreal, the subjects are fascinating for their own sake, or if the unreality were the result of mythic-expressionist distortion, then the secondary interests of mannerist style and treatment in an author like Achilleus Tatios would combine to give him real importance. But as it is, the very heart and core of his subject is vitiated by naked quest for distraction; ancient Romance is basically escapist entertainment literature.

As Albin Lesky remarks, in Greek Romance an altered sense for life is expressed.[1] The world had long since ceased to be grasped and interpreted within the framework of the traditional myths. The city-state does not exist as a focus of significance for the ordinary citizen. Even Greek culture as a whole has lost the power to provide a framework, an orientation for the life of an

individual: in the centuries of Rome's control, Greek history is
ancient history. As for Rome itself, it is too far away; the individual in the provinces can have no way of direct identification
with its meaning. The consequence of this is that for the great
majority of individuals ordinary life in the towns was trivialized.

If the ordinary citizens had been philosophers, they could
have searched for the cosmic significance in the details amid
which they lived. If they had been Christians, the divine meaning
in the quotidian would have been available to them. But as it
was, they were stranded without any method of breaking through
to that meaning. And the loss of meaning in the quotidian led to
the imaginative flight from it. So it is that Heliodoros, for example, despite his quest for striking detail, never makes his detail
fully alive, and must give it the external animation of his rhetoric.
Even the religious significance of his story is *worked into* the
events. The divine power shapes the action by *external* control.
There is no grounding of that significance in the detail; it is not
seen through the detail; it does not spring from the detail.

Erich Auerbach, in a brilliant chapter in *Mimesis*, examines
the way in which the spiritual drought of the later Roman Empire is reflected in the contorted sensationalism of some of its
Latin *prosateurs*.[2] Achilleus Tatios and Heliodoros would have
given him the material for another chapter dealing with the
Greek parallels.

Now it was a further thesis of Auerbach that the experience
of the Bible was responsible for the movement toward a serious
(non-satiric, non-comic) representation of ordinary existence in
Western literature, and that this can be demonstrated on the level
of style.[3] In general, the thesis is surely sound. But *Daphnis and
Chloe* is *one* work of pagan literature where a similar achievement is made: the detail of ordinary existence is not only presented but celebrated, and celebrated because of the ultimate
significance perceived in that detail.

It is possible to account for this side of the work's success in
almost botanical terms: *Daphnis and Chloe* is a hybrid. (It is
perhaps some corroboration of this account that the other two
great "novels" of antiquity—those by Apuleius and Petronius—
are also clearly hybrids.) In a hybrid each stock contributes some
virtue missing in the other. So in the case of Longus, the pastoral

(thanks to the mimic-realistic tradition it springs from) enables a steady and loving reference to milk pails, myrtle berries, erotic frisking of goats, birds, bees, and blossoms, fountains, fields, caves, pine trees, pan-pipes, cicadas chirping, soft breezes, and the scent of fruit. It also enables an indirect or allusive, sometimes ironic treatment of erotic and poetic themes.

What does Romance contribute? Obviously it brings a fuller action, a plot with deeper involvement—mechanical and sensational though it may be—with the vicissitudes of life. But above all, it brings the *motif* of divine providence, of a religious meaning associated with events. But the trouble with Romance—the trouble even with Heliodoros, the most valuable of the group— was that this significance was attached *ab extra;* it was a devotional decal glued to one's automobile windshield.

I *Syncretist Natural Godhead*

How does Longus, by contrast, ground the divinity in the detail? How does the divinity dwell within the action? The god who lives in the story of Daphnis and Chloe is not Artemis or Isis, but Eros, and not just the Eros who had been conventionalized in Cupid. As the god himself says in his epiphany: "I'm not really a boy, even if I seem to be; I'm older than Kronos and the whole of time itself" (II 5). This is the cosmic Eros of Hesiodic, Orphic, and philosophical traditions. But the age is one of syncretism, and H. O. Chalk has demonstrated in detail how this Eros is fused with other gods of the story, particularly Dionysos. The Dionysian fusion strengthens the association (likely in any case) of Eros with the processes and powers of nature. The result is immediately that all the detail in the book, that is to say, all the natural detail, serves to show forth the god. Whereas in Heliodoros and the others the description was laid on, either as rhetorical show piece or mere quest for the exotic, here in Longus all description is functional; it harmonizes with the general conception. In fact (as discussed earlier), the book as a whole is conceived under the metaphor of an *ekphrasis,* or description:

When I was hunting in Lesbos, I saw in a grove sacred to the Nymphs the fairest sight I ever saw: a painted picture [literally, "icon"], a story [the word *historia* has an undertone of "investigation"] of Eros . . . a yearning came over me to write an equivalent to the picture.

So I hunted out an interpreter ["exegete"] and wrought these four
volumes as an offering to Eros, the Nymphs, and Pan, and as . . .
(*Proemium*)

As a parallel illustration of the religious-symbolic employment
of the *ekphrasis*, compare the beginning of the *Painting* (*pinax*)
by pseudo-Kebes—a work probably written in the century previous to Longus:[4]

We chanced to be strolling in the sanctuary of Kronos, looking at the
many gifts dedicated to the gods—and especially at a certain tablet
in front of the temple. It had a curious picture with a subject all its
own, impossible for us to make out. For it seemed to be neither a city,
nor any army camp, yet it was an enclosure, with two smaller en-
closures inside. At the outside gate, a great mob appeared to be
standing. Within was a crowd of women. At the entrance an old man
stood in the guise of one giving instructions to the throng as it entered.

(In the sequel, an elderly man comes up to the temple visitors
and explains the picture at length; it turns out to be an elaborate
philosophico-religious allegory.)

The reader needs more than just the assertion that the descriptive natural detail of *Daphnis and Chloe* reveals the god. The
particular force of particular details, so far as possible, should
be made clear to him. First, he needs some notion of how far the
syncretism of the times could go. Here is a sample; Isis is speaking
in her epiphany to Lucius in Apuleius' *Metamorphoses*:

Lo, here am I, Lucius, summoned by your prayers. I am mother of
the universe, mistress of all the elements, the firstborn of all the ages,
highest of gods, queen of the dead, first among the heavenly ones, the
summary revelation of all gods and goddesses. With my will I control
the bright summits of heaven, the beneficial breezes of the sea, the
silences of the mourned-for dead. My sole and single godhead the
entire world reveres under manifold aspects, diverse rites, and many
names.   (*Metamorphoses* XI 5)

After this, the reader should not be surprised to find one *persona*
of the supreme divinity merging into another and a state of
affairs reached where "the old myths seemed capable of every
conceivable interpretation and everything a symbol of everything
else."[5]

Second, the reader should note some literary expression elsewhere of the divine immanence in the minute processes of the
natural world: "the force that through the green fuse drives the
flower." [6] Earlier poets and philosophers (Empedokles, Euripides,
and Marcus Aurelius, for example) in varying degrees would
serve to illustrate. But a very close analogue, both in thought
and in date, deserves special citation; the poet is describing
Venus:

> She decks the reddening year with flower jewels;
> She drives the buds which swell under the spring breeze
> into passionate blossom; she scatters the waters
> of the shining dew, left by the night air
> . . . .
> She guides and engenders from within by hidden powers,
> as her breath pervades the veins and mind.
> Throughout the sky and land and sea below
> along the paths which bear the seed,
> she diffuses a passionate warmth to prepare her way,
> and bids the world learn the roads to birth.
>
>   (*Pervigilium Veneris*, from text as in *Oxford Book of
>   Latin Verse*, pp. 375ff.)

But this is just preparatory stage setting.

II *Symbols*

For the full demonstration of Longus' intricate nature symbolism let us begin with the nomenclature of the story. As Lindsay points out, the names of the major figures are significant:[7]

Daphnis not only connotes the legendary proto-herdsman; in
a context where other major names carry vegetation symbolism,
the name also suggests the laurel (and myths had developed
which associated both Daphnis and Daphne with the plant).

Chloe means the "first green shoot of plants in the spring"[8]
and, among other things, was used as a cult title for Demeter
("Earth-Mother," possibly) at Athens. ("Chloe," incidentally, is
cognate with the name for the greenish gas chlorine.)

Lamon, among the group of Daphnis and Chloe and their
foster parents, is a puzzling departure from the pattern. The
name is said by Lindsay to come from the pastoral poets, but I
have not located it thus far.

Myrtale is derived from the word for myrtle, a plant with special religious significance, associated with both Aphrodite and Dionysos.[9]

Dryas is derived from *drys*, "oak" (and cognate with English "tree"). Apart from an association with Dryads (tree nymphs), there is also the primordial sacredness of the oak tree itself, and its function in the story as the regular meeting place for Daphnis and Chloe.

Nape means "dell," or "glen."

Dionysophanes is an astonishingly direct religious clue. The name belongs to the realm of occult syncretism. According to the traditional (but not necessarily correct) ancient etymology it literally means "Dionysos in his advent." "Phanes" was also used by the Orphics as a separate name, alternate to Dionysos and to Eros, to refer to the "father of all gods." [10]

Now Eros and Dionysos are both prominent divinities in Longus. What about the other prominent god—Pan? Here is an *Orphic Hymn* to Pan which shows how easily the Pan of Longus can and should be regarded as simply the specifically pastoral *persona* of the one supreme god. Note amid the exuberant stream of epithets how many of them are related to *Daphnis and Chloe:*

> I invoke mighty Pan, shepherd-lawyer, totality [*sympan*]
>   of the universe;
> heaven and sea and all-queen earth
> and deathless fire (for these are the limbs of Pan).
> Come, blessed, frolicker, runner-in-circles, you who
>   sit with the Seasons,
> goat-foot, Bacchic reveler, lover of the mystic trance,
>   dweller in the open starry fields,
> warbling the harmony of the universe with your sportive
>   song,
> defender from visions, terrible among mortal fears [?]
> delighting in goatherds and cowherds among the springs,
> sharpshooter, hunter, dear to Echo, dancing-partner to
>   Nymphs,
> source of all growth, all-begetter, many-named god,
> universe-ruler, giver of increase, light-bringer, fruit-
>   ful Healer,
> cave-lover, terrible in anger, the true horned Zeus.
>   (*Orphic Hymn* XI 1–12 Quandt)

(Lest it be thought that the Nymphs were slighted by the Orphics, note that they have their own hymn, LI, which I shall reluctantly omit here.)

A warning should be issued that Longus is not to be pinned down as a member of a particular cult; the most one dare say is that, for literary purposes, he is employing the symbolic and associative possibilities which the religious situation in late pagan antiquity provided. (One suggestion, however, is that Longus was a Dionysian priest on Lesbos, the island which was reputed the final resting place of Orpheus' severed, floating head, and where it was established in a shrine of Dionysos.) [11]

Now, after all these preliminaries, how does the god live in the details? I depend in the following upon Chalk's epochal article, of which I can provide only a most imperfect review of the relevant points: [12] Eros is in the first place symbolically associated with the flowing water (fountains, rivers, even the sea) which sustains the vitality of nature. Among the many places where water bears the divine, that in Philetas' garden is most explicit: characteristically, the mysticism is given a playful, witty twist by representing the Eros-sprung vegetative vitality as imparted by way of his bathing effluvia. (The Nymphs, who are in charge of fountains and streams, are his handmaids.)

Eros also is winged; the wings may derive ultimately from a very early tendency to depict spiritual powers in this way; but in Orphic cosmogony, Eros was hatched from a primal cosmic egg, and in a number of other ways his connections with birds lay ready to hand. (Thrushes, for example, were thought to be an aphrodisiac food.) The connection is exploited by Aristophanes in a famous burlesque cosmogony which he puts in the mouth of his bird chorus in the *Birds:*

> Black-winged Night first of all gives birth to a windy
> egg
> from which, as seasons rolled, the lovely Eros sprouted,
> flashing with golden wings on his back, like swift
> wind-wheels.
>
> (*Birds* 695–97)

So it is more than a demonstration of naïveté when Daphnis and Chloe ask Philetas whether Eros is a boy or a bird. And when birds are present in the story, Longus has usually planned for them to intimate the divine.

The natural music of the birds (Eros is said to have a voice sweeter than the songbirds) and the shepherd music on the pan-pipes is related to the conception of music as a reflection of the cosmic order. Thus the shepherd-poet tradition of the pastoral is deepened to the image of shepherd as an embodiment of the musical universal god. Pan's piping—as the *Orphic Hymn* quoted above illustrates—was taken as a form of the harmony of the All (*pan*). Some particularly striking instances of the "power of music" in a natural-cosmic way are: the rescue of Daphnis from the pirates by the pipe music; the supernatural piping which was heard during the rescue of Chloe from the Methymnaean navy; and the ability of Daphnis to make his flock dance variously in response to his various piping.[13]

III *Vegetation*

A realm of detail in the story which is particularly rich in symbolic suggestion is that of the vegetation. Myrtle, pomegra-nate, ivy, vine, oak, and pine are all closely associated with one or all of the Eros-Dionysos-Pan complex. For example, to the an-cient reader, the berried ivy suddenly appearing on the horns of the stolen goats was a clear signal of the onset of overwhelming punitive power of Dionysos against those who had sinned against him. The *locus classicus* for such imagery is the *Homeric Hymn* to Dionysos.[14] The pine with which Chloe suddenly appears crowned suggests in the first instance Pan, who is mythologically associated with the pine in a story alluded to at several points.[15]

Apart from the specific vegetable symbolism, gardens as a whole have a religious-symbolic character in the story. The gar-dens of Philetas and Dionysophanes are clearly hallowed by divine presence: Eros in person in the one; the shrine of Dionysos in the other. The link between gods of natural power and gardens is an easy one. An early involvement of Eros with gardens is in the following fragment from Ibykos:

> In spring the quinces
> and pomegranates (nourished
> from streams in the unspoiled
> garden of the Nymphs) and vine-buds
> swelling under the shady

leaves surge forth. But for me, Eros
never sleeps . . . [i.e., is active even in wintry old age].
(Ibykos No. 5 in *Melici Graeci,* Page)

An instructive contrast to Longus' symbolic-religious treatment
of gardens can be found in the otherwise similar gardens of two
of his approximate contemporaries. Alkiphron in his account of
a country outing by some courtesans and their lovers uses his
garden description merely to give us the setting of a glorified
playboy den, a backdrop for sheer Aphrodisianism:

A short way off from the country-house was a rock roofed over by
laurels and plane trees; on either side were myrtle shrubs; ivy en-
circled it, clinging to its surface as if woven there. Pure water trickled
down from it. Beneath its projections some statues of the Nymphs
were set up, and Pan was peeping over as if spying on the Naiads.
(IV 13, Benner and Fobes)

The garden in Achilleus Tatios (I 15) is described at length and
has some superficial resemblances to Longus, especially to Dionysophanes' garden and its elaborate symmetrical design, but the
purely rhetorical-descriptive intent of the passage is patent:
there are no shreds of symbolism and significance which might
tie it to the rest of the story.

The vegetation links establish another important feature of the
religious symbolism of the book. It is not only the appearance of
particular plants at various points, or their ensemble in the garden: Longus also integrates the natural life-rhythm of vegetation
into the sequence of his plot in a way that deepens the significance of his story. The nature-gods, since associated with vegetation, were conceived of as participating with nature in the
wintry death of the year and its vernal rebirth.

With the topic of dying-and-rising gods, we approach an area
of literary interpretation where more than ordinary discretion is
desirable. There is a school of scholarship on the Romances which
sees their fundamental significance (and origin) in some form
of mystery religion concerned with such gods, and claims that
the Romances employ a symbolism that deliberately evokes the
ritual of the worship of these gods, particularly the ritual of
initiation.[16] For the other Romances I join those who doubt that
any such explicit significance is basic.

For *Daphnis and Chloe*, however, I find it impossible to doubt
that mystery gods and mystery ritual are deeply involved. As
Chalk and others have pointed out, Longus is at pains to associate the rhythm of human experience with the natural rhythm of
the seasons, and he has descriptively clothed both with language
suggestive of the underlying rhythms of the divine life which
rules both man and nature.[17] I shall make three illustrations:

Daphnis and Chloe are partly embodiments of the divinities
whom they serve. The association begins with the birth stories.
It is a commonplace in New Comedy for foundlings to be rescued
by shepherds, and although such stories in their mythical form
clearly are related to births of gods and demigods (ultimately
the newborn vegetation gods of the new year), nevertheless, the
frequency of the theme in comedy and elsewhere forbids assign-
ing it religious significance as such. In Longus, however, the case
is different; consider the details: Daphnis is found in an oak-
wood (*drymos;* the word is related to "Dryas") with ivy covering
the ground; a goat was nursing him. This last detail is important:
the miraculous preservation by animal nurse of the newborn god
or hero exposed in the wilds is a story told in a number of forms
in antiquity, as I have already mentioned in Chapter 2. In one
version, Zeus himself was suckled by the goat Amaltheia. Now
Daphnis, to be sure, may be said to deserve such a birth sheerly
because his name associates him with the legendary hero-patron
of shepherds, but the symbolic involvement of nature gods here
in the oak and ivy (and elsewhere in the story) gives to his birth
a penumbra of the annual divine rebirth.

A second example: The autumnal preparation for the arrival of
Dionysophanes, the anxiety of Daphnis and Chloe, the overtones
of test and ordeal, especially the elaborate development of the
garden episode (which is explicitly linked to Dionysos by the
presence of his shrine)—these are all persuasively interpreted
by Chalk to suggest the experience of the epiphany of the god,
together with the natural and the ritual-initiatory death which is
the autumnal phase of the divine life-cycle.

One of the clearest instances of the fusion achieved by Longus
of the natural, human, and divine cycles is the episode of the
winter bird-catching near the beginning of Book III. Let us consider it in somewhat greater detail, so as to illustrate the ease and
care with which Longus arranges his symbolic combinations.

After the initial description of the wintry scene and the relaxed indoor life of the peasantry, Daphnis and Chloe are separated out as missing their past delights, spending their time sorrowfully. "They waited for the spring season as a rebirth from death" (III 4). "Rebirth from death" is a phrase drawn from the language of the mystery religions and can be applied literally only to the death and life of the god, but it is obviously drawn into connection with the human and natural levels here.

The device contrived by Daphnis to maintain at least some contact with Chloe during this dark season is intimately involved with the imagery of the latent divine powers of regeneration: the spot he picks for his bird-catching has two large myrtle shrubs, with ivy springing up in between. The ivy spreads out on each side over the myrtle, like a vine, making a sort of bower. Down from the ivy hangs a great cluster of its berries, like a cluster of grapes. The winter birds, as many as feed on the ivy and myrtle berries, come there to feed.

A further significance of the passage is less easily demonstrable to the skeptical. To begin with, it is one of three major passages descriptive of a vegetation scene; it is located midway between Philetas' description of his own garden in Book II and the description of the garden of Dionysophanes in Book IV. The two major gardens are meant to be associated, not only by the explicit divine-show for which each is the setting, but also by many shared descriptive features. The site of the winter bird-feeding then functions as a sparse wintry equivalent: it is all that can survive of the autumnal abundance of the other two; it is a kind of garden for the god in his hidden form (a *deus absconditus,* as it were).

The interconnection between the three scenes is further strengthened by the distribution of themes: in the first garden, where many birds gather, Philetas spots Eros as an intruder and tries to catch him lest he break down the flowers. But Eros eludes him like a bird (his voice, when he speaks, is more beautiful than nightingale, swallow, or swan) and finally disappears up through the tree branches like the young nightingale, after Philetas has caught a glimpse of his wings. Now, out of these features of the first garden, the winter scene inherits the bird-catching, while the damage done to a garden by an intruder comes in Dionysophanes' garden in Book IV. (No birds appear in connection with the latter garden.) Furthermore, in both winter scene and the garden in Book IV there is the peculiar feature of a cluster of ivy berries which is said to resemble a cluster of grapes.[18]

The religious significance of the winter scene becomes fully explicit at last when Daphnis joins with Chloe and her family in the vine-crowned wine-drinking celebration of the winter Diony-sos rites—rites which invoked that god who could bring back the spring.

Earlier in this chapter I stated that the Romantic theme of Providence is given a hybrid fusion by Longus with the natural detail of the pastoral, the result being a celebration of the god *in* nature. Now that we have seen some specific instances of the fusion, once more let me claim that it is from this that the theme of benign control of human affairs acquires a persuasiveness and imaginative plausibility which the other Romances, in their lack of an organic harmony of nature, man, and god, do not achieve. Longus is the only pagan Greek who shows us Providence in such a form that we might be willing to believe, after all, that it is manifest even "in the fall of a sparrow"—or in "the leaves flying in the wind."

CHAPTER 7

Soundings

WE have now inventoried the sources upon which Longus allusively draws far enough that it should be possible to dip in at any point in the work and savor the various ingredients in their coalescence. So before going further in the total assessment of the novel, it is time to sample the results to this point. Let us conduct the review in two ways, extensively and intensively. Extensively, I shall repeat the salient points of the plot summary given at the beginning of the book, this time including in parentheses enough of an abbreviated annotation to indicate what various threads have been woven into the fabric. The reader can then judge for himself whether my claim was correct that the mere summary told essentially nothing about the true character of the work. Then, intensively, I shall select a major passage from the novel and attempt to show how, down to the finest detail, the complex weaving continues.

I *Full-Color Summary*

Book I. On the island Lesbos (associated with supreme love poetry and a cult of Dionysos) near the city Mitylene (Sappho's birthplace) in the old days before Roman domination (a convention of Greek Romance, but here especially appropriate to the Golden Age idealization and the inclusive gesture toward the Greek literary tradition) a wealthy man had a country estate (immediately evokes the themes of New Comedy: rich/poor, free/slave, city/country; furthermore, provides the cornerstone for the pastoral treatment). One of his goatherds found one day in an ivy-covered glade a goat suckling a baby boy (ivy: Dionysos; goat: Pan; scene suggests birth stories in New Comedy, but behind that and even more, births of gods and heroes; providential care for the child will be thematic). He took the baby home to his wife Myrtale; they named it Daphnis (both names have

vegetation reference; Daphnis also suggests the legendary herdsman). Two years later the shepherd Dryas (name) found a
sheep suckling a baby girl near a fountain (fountains are thematic) in a cave of the Nymphs (the pastoral amoebeic parallelism is now complete: Pan/Nymphs, goatherd/shepherd, goat/
sheep, boy/girl—and it will be exploited in the plot).

When Daphnis was fifteen and Chloe thirteen (natural time
for the natural discovery of Eros), Lamon and Dryas had the
same dream (the oracular dream as a way of initiating action is
an old element of Greek storytelling) [1] of Daphnis and Chloe
delivered to a winged boy (the conventional boy-Eros of Greek
love poetry) who bade them become herdsmen (mystical-natural
significance in the link between love and herds will be summed
up in the formula Eros the Shepherd; divine harmony of man
and nature). Daphnis and Chloe took to the fields in the spring
(the birth of the year and the birth of their love: coordination
of human and natural rhythm; pastoral themes are now fully
installed). They imitate the play of nature (their whole story
will body forth the mimetically achieved human harmony with
nature).

The wolf's incursions (a thematic form which some apparent
obstacles to the love of Daphnis and Chloe will take: cf. Dorkon's
wolf disguise, and the etymology of "Lykainion"). The bath at
the Nymphs' spring (ritual ablution and the infusion of Eros).
Chloe's new interest in Daphnis (totally welcome modulation of
the Romance topos of love at first sight). Her ignorance of its true
nature (artificial pastoral naïveté and part of the ritual initiatory
sequence). Dorkon's suit to Chloe (the Romance convention of
interference from a seasoned lover). Debate between Dorkon
and Daphnis, with kiss as prize (mixture of pastoral agon and
Second Sophistic rhetoric). Effect of Chloe's kiss (a topos in love
poetry). Digression on the mourning dove (digression is conventional with Romance; here, unconventionally, there is an implicit
relation to the actual plot). Pirate raid (a Romance convention).
Dorkon's rehabilitation (pastoral lenience). Power of pan-pipes
over the stolen herd (cosmic Pan music). Comic version of rescue
(pastoral sportiveness injected into Romance melodrama). Ride
to shore after the kidnap (suggests stories associated with Dionysos).[2]

Book II. Fall vintage (good time for year-god epiphany, es-

pecially Dionysian). Visit from Philetas (name recalls a founder
of Hellenistic love poetry and teacher of Theokritos) who tells of
Eros' appearance and message. Party boys on a hunt (New
Comedy; city irruption into country). Goat nibbles hawser, etc.
(playful elaboration of "haphazard" causal sequence beloved of
Romance). Methymnaean incursion, leading to capture of Chloe
(Romance convention). Divine wrath against fleet (tradition of
Dionysian revenge on the impious,[3] and Pan-ic fear in armies).
At family religious celebration party (New Comedy) mimic
dances (Xenophon's *Symposium*).[4] Philetas gives pipes to Daph-
nis (pastoral convention of master-pupil musical hand-me-down).[5]

   Book III. Pocket war between Mitylene and Methymna (mock
bow to Romance convention). Winter (ritual dead season).
Daphnis' bird-catching (clinging to erotic clues to help get
through the hard times; garden-surrogate). Lykainion (in addition to the wolf theme and the Romantic topos of Potiphar's
Wife: from New Comedy, the kindly, helpful hetaira). Chloe's
virginity preserved (ritual-initiatory requirement of purity).
Daphnis' difficulty with herdsman-rivals (New Comedy). Dream
of the Nymphs and discovery of the purse (mock-completion of
marriage via a set of New Comedy themes). Postponement of
marriage until master's arrival (divine autumnal advent, parallel-
ing that in Book II; approach of ritual ordeal).

   Book IV. Dionysophanes (name). The despoiling of the garden (mystical death and ordeal of nature, man, and god; balance
with Philetas' garden in Book II). Astylos and Gnathon (New
Comedy types). Gnathon's designs on Daphnis; Lampis' on
Chloe (final versions of Romance topos of the rival; special emphasis, in this context, on the unnaturalness of Gnathon; divine
providence at work: the one rival defeats himself and the other).
Restoration of Daphnis and Chloe; emancipation of foster parents;
wedding (regular New Comedy and Romance endings). Life
thereafter in the fields (Arcadian-pastoral deflection).

II *Closeup*

Book II 3–7:

   As they were having their fun, an old man came upon them,[a]
clothed in a goatskin, shod in rough leather, and wearing a shepherd's
pouch—an old one. He sat down nearby and said, "Children, I am
old Philetas.[b] I have often sung to these Nymphs here, often piped

to Pan over there, and led many cattle sheerly by my music.^c I am
here to reveal what I have seen, and report what I have heard.^d I
have a garden—my own handiwork: after I grew too old to be shepherd, I managed to set it out. All that each season brings, it bears: in
spring, roses, lilies, hyacinth, and both violets; in summer, poppies,
pears, and all apples; and now, grapes, figs, pomegranates, and green
myrtle. Flocks of birds gather in this garden at dawn, some to feed,
some to sing. For they find shelter and shade, and the streams of three
springs. Take away the fence, and you will think you're in a grove." ^e

    a. "came upon them": the verb in Greek is associated with
dream visions and other significant encounters (for example, the
appearance of the Laws to Socrates at the climax of Plato's *Krito*).
"An old man" prepares Philetas' role as teacher.
    b. "Philetas": a founder of Hellenistic love poetry, teacher of
Theokritos, leader of a poetic circle.
    c. This description of himself attaches him to the pastoral con-
vention of shepherd as poet; further, to the theme of mystical-
musical cosmic harmony which controls nature (cf. the other
passages of musical herd control).
    d. "To reveal . . . and report": the Greek verbs *menuein* and
apangellein suggest religious revelation, perhaps in ritual context.
    e. The religious significance of the garden, with its plants, birds,
and fountains, has been discussed earlier. Note that the association with the garden in Book IV is strengthened by abundant
parallels in the plant life, and in the reference to the (dry-stone)
fence: *haimasia* occurs only in these two passages.

    Now today, when I went in there around noon,^a under the myrtle
and pomegranate trees I saw a boy with those fruits in his hands—
white as milk, tawny as fire, gleaming as if fresh from the bath.^b He
had no clothes, no companions; frisking around and plucking the fruit
from his own garden, he seemed.^c So I rushed to catch him; I was
afraid the brash boy would break the branches.^d But he skipped away
light and easy, running under the roses or hiding under the poppies,
like a partridge chick.^e Many a time I have worn myself out chasing
the unweaned kids, and many a time I have struggled after the new
lambs, but *here* was something baffling and elusive.^f

    a. Noon in the countryside is a numinous time, associated par-
ticularly with Pan. It was at noon that the Methymnaean com-
mander mysteriously fell asleep and had his dream of Pan.

b. The naked beauty of the boy is part of the conventional representation of Eros.

c. The irony of Philetas' ignorance of the boy's true identity is a theme in his narrative. Here: "as if plucking the fruit from his own garden"—in fact it is his own garden, as will be clear by the end.

d. This fear that the intruder will wantonly destroy the plants foreshadows Lampis' destructiveness in Book IV. There is also perhaps here a nuance of the violence which is another aspect of the divine activity, and which Chalk interprets in such things as Dorkon's behavior, the story of Echo, and the scenes depicted on the shrine of Dionysos in the middle of the garden in Book IV.[6]

e. Here begins the association of Eros with birds.

f. Philetas' bafflement is characteristic in stories of attempted human aggression upon the gods. Of particular relevance to Longus (though tragedy has become comedy) is the account of Pentheus' furious frustration when trying to imprison Dionysos, in Euripides' *Bakchai* 616ff. (Jacob wrestling with the angel is a Hebraic counterpart.)

At last, weary with an old man's weariness, leaning on my stick and watching so he wouldn't get past me, I asked him which house he came from and what he meant by stealing fruit from other people's gardens.[a] But he didn't answer; he just came up close and started laughing seductively while he pelted me with myrtle berries and somehow charmed me out of my anger.[b] In fact, I found myself begging him to come up close and not to worry; I swore by the myrtles I would let him go safe and give him the fruit, and also let him pick the trees and pluck the flowers forever, if he would let me kiss him only once.

a. The theme of ironic ignorance is continued.

b. The traditional witchery of the boy Eros, here reinforced by his characteristic laughter, and by the magical-ritual pelting with the love-token myrtle berries (those berries on which the birds will feed in the winter fowling scene).

At this he laughed like a flute, then spoke in a voice beyond the swallow or nightingale, or even the aged swan old as I:[a] "Kissing you, Philetas, is more than easy for me;[b] I am more eager for kisses than you are for youth. But is this a gift that fits your time of life? One kiss, and old age won't keep you from chasing me.ᶜ And it is hard for a hawk or eagle or even a swifter bird to catch me.ᵈ You should know I am not a boy, though I seem like one: I am older than Kronos and all time.ᵉ I have known you ever since you were a boy and tended the wide flock in that meadow over there, and I sat beside you when you piped near those beeches and were in love with Amaryllis.ᶠ I was right next to the girl, and you didn't see me.ᵍ Through me you won her, and now you have fine children: herdsmen and farmers."ʰ

    a. Eros as superbird, here in his voice.
    b. "Kissing," in the Greek (*philesai*), puns on "Philetas."
    c. The stimulus of a kiss is a love poet's topos, and the figure of the old man uncomfortably or inappropriately in love is also part of the poetic tradition, particularly in Ibykos and Anakreon.
    d. Superbird again.
    e. Here the Hesiodic, philosophic, and—particularly—Orphic conception of Eros as primal source of gods and cosmos is juxtaposed with the pretty boy of the love poets. There is a pun on "Kronos" and "time" (*chronos*) which reflects an identification between the two which was made in post-classical times (and is presumably the origin of our Old Father Time).[7]
    f. A clear allusion to Vergil's *First Eclogue:*

> Tityrus, reclining under cover of the broad beech tree
> you devote yourself to the woodland muse with your small
>   pipe
> . . . .
> you teach the forest to re-echo the name of lovely
>   Amaryllis.
>   (Vergil, *Eclogue* I 1ff.)

This connection is further strengthened later on, in II 8, when Philetas says, "I praised Echo for calling out after me the name of Amaryllis." (Both Vergil and Longus, however, may have appropriated from poetry of Philetas now lost. Cf. Philetas, fr. 14 in J. V. Powell, *Collectanea Alexandrina*.)
    g. The hidden presence of the god: a benign version of blindness such as that of Pentheus to the presence of Dionysos; for example, in *Bakchai* 498–502:

D: The god himself will free me when I wish.
P: If you can manage to call him after you've made your escape.
D: He is here right now and sees what I endure.
P: Just where is he? I can't make him out.
D: He is with me. But your impiety blocks your sight.

h. The god's providential care, soon to be proclaimed for Daphnis and Chloe.

"So now I am shepherd of Daphnis and Chloe,[a] and after I bring them together at dawn, I come to your garden to enjoy the flowers and trees and to bathe in these springs. From this the flowers and trees get their beauty: their water comes from my bath.[b] You will find no branches broken, no fruit stolen, no flower trampled, no fountain roiled. Goodbye; be glad: among old men only you have seen this child."

Then he hopped to the myrtle boughs, like a nestling nightingale, and crept from branch to branch through the leaves to the top.[c] I saw the wings at his shoulders, and the bow between the wings, and then both these and he were gone.[d] If my gray head is worth anything, if my brain is not just silly from antiquity, you have been signed over to Eros, my dears, and Eros cares.

a. This statement points to the cult title he will later receive: "Eros the Shepherd" (IV 39), a title related to the themes of providential care and of pastoral nature-god. (Compare the Christian development of the pastoral metaphor, as in the hymn "The King of Love My Shepherd Is.")

b. Fountains are thematic sites of erotic power; here Love's irrigation of nature is wittily said to come from his bath water, a sophistic-pastoral conceit.

c. Compare Theokritos XV 120–22:

> . . . and the young Erotes fly overhead
> like nightingale chicks flying over a tree from branch
> to branch
> as they try out their growing wings.

d. The conventional picture of the boy-Eros is now completed by bow and wings.

In addition to these individual points, the entire episode thus

far is a free-swinging inversion of passages from the pastoral
poets Bion and Moschos. As a measure of Longus' alchemy, I
reproduce Bion here:

> A young bird-catcher, hunting birds
> in a grove, saw Eros the wild
> sitting on a boxtree branch. He was delighted
> at his find, for the bird was a big one, he thought.
> Tying all his lime-reeds together
> he tried to ambush Eros, who was hopping here and there.
> Then, getting angry because he had no luck,
> he threw the reeds away and went over to an old plowman
> who had taught him the craft of bird-catching, and he
>   told his trouble
> and pointed out Eros where he sat. But the old man
> smiled, shook his head, and answered the boy:
> "You can save yourself the trouble of hunting that bird.
> Keep clear of it; it's a wild evil thing. You're for-
>   tunate
> so long as you haven't caught it. But when you get to
>   be a man,
> this one who jumps around to escape you will come
> of his own accord and land on your head."

> (Bion XIII Gow)

They were as pleased as if they had heard a story, not just a report,[a] and they asked what was Eros—a boy or a bird,[b] and what
could he do? So Philetas told them, "Eros is a god; young, fair, and
flying. That's why he loves the young, chases the fair, and fits out
souls with wings.[c] He has more power than even Zeus.[d] He rules
the elements[e] and rules the stars; he rules the gods who are his peers:
not even you are such rulers over your goats and sheep.[f] All flowers
are his works; he made these trees; for him the rivers flow and the
winds blow." [g]

a. It is hard to catch the precise point of the contrast here.
(The Greek words are *mythos* and *logos*.) On the surface it is
the pleasure of story as against mere information. But there is
the further suggestion of myth (in the strong sense) over against
abstract philosophizing or theologizing. (Perhaps the contrast is
even between myth as religiously edifying, as against a mere
story.) Pan's declaration to the general Bryaxis (see the end of

the quotation in Chapter I) [8] about the "maid whom Eros has chosen as heroine for his tale" (literally "myth") should be associated.

b. Here the ignorance of Daphnis and Chloe is artificial and ritually uninitiated. The question "boy or bird?" prepares for the *tertium quid* of Philetas' answer: "a *god*." And Philetas thereupon appropriately assumes the role of theologian. ("Boy, bird, and god" sum up the human, natural, and divine realms with which the book as a whole is occupied.)

c. This probably glances at Plato's doctrine of the mystical-philosophical insight which erotic passion can bestow:

Whenever [the philosophically disposed person] beholds a godlike face or some bodily form which is a fair image of [the transcendent] Beauty, first a shudder comes over him. . . . Then he venerates the object of his contemplation like a god, and if he had no fear of being thought violently insane, he would offer sacrifice to the boy he loves as if he were a holy statue. After he has beheld and the shudder is gone, a sweat and a strange fever seize him. For he receives the effusion of the beauty through his eyes and is warmed where the nourishing of his soul's wings takes place. The warmth melts the passageways of growth, which have long been hardened and closed over so nothing could sprout. And now nourishment flows in, and the wing-stalk swells and surges out from the root, spreading underneath the entire framework of the soul. For long ago it was feathered all over. (*Phaidros* 251 a–b)

d. The pre-eminent power of Eros, even over the other gods, is a long-standing poetic topos.

e. "The elements" (*stoicheia*)—a technical philosophical term, perhaps suggesting Orphic cosmology.[9]

f. Pastoral anticlimax, yet suggesting Daphnis and Chloe as divine surrogates.

g. For all this assertion of supreme cosmic power, compare the passage quoted earlier from Apuleius, where Isis speaks of herself.

Throughout this comment I have ignored most of the purely stylistic features of the passage, but perhaps even in the translation the persistent grouping of parallel phrases in pairs and

triads is self-evident. What does not come through in a translation for the most part is the use of *rhythmic* parallels and rhyme,
not to mention the variegated effects of sheer prose rhythm and
word sound outside the parallels and the rhymes.

CHAPTER 8

Hybrid Virtues II: Arcadia

THUS far we have explored the mutual enrichment which Longus achieved by combining the neutral detail of the pastoral with the religious motif and more inclusive action structure of the Romance. But there is another effect of the fusion of the two genres of pastoral mime and Romance in *Daphnis and Chloe:* each genre contributes its own kind of idealization. The pastoral poetry of Theokritos, although it embodied a tradition of vivid commonplace detail, was never fully realistic. The setting was always to some degree idealized. But the same was not always true of the shepherds and shepherdesses who peopled that setting: insofar as they are characterized, many are mildly ridiculous, or at least ordinary in their affections and spites.[1] Romance, on the other hand, by definition has a hero and heroine quite excessively ideal.

In Longus the two kinds of idealization combine perfectly. The gain is noticed especially in the case of the two lovers. In the young goatherd and shepherdess, the tedious urban virtue of the other Romances is transformed into sheer innocence, inexperience, and natural good temper.

Now it is true that an exaltation of the pastoral personages had already become standard at an earlier point in the pastoral tradition; namely, in Vergil's *Eclogues.* Bruno Snell has described how Vergil pulled the tradition toward an idealized epic seriousness by setting his poems in the "invented" legendary landscape of Arcadia and by bringing the gods into close contact with the figures, whose passions are now treated seriously, almost tragically—in contrast to the frequent Theokritean objectivity and comedy.[2] But the development in Vergil is characteristically Roman. Although Longus clearly knew Vergil's work, if he took all this modification of the pastoral from him, he reinfused the Theokritean rustic clowning, good cheer, and much else.

Whatever the relationship, both authors at any rate have in common a pastoral utopianism, one furthermore which is distinguished from that in Dion's *Euboean Discourse* in that the utopia retains a distant legendary magic from the past, where gods are still capable of moving among men; it is not (as with Dion) a contemporary "Elsewhere" (or "Nowhere"). For Daphnis and Chloe, as earlier expounded, part of the idealized enhancement comes from their involvement in a symbolic and mythical initiation sequence: they are naïve and innocent not just because pastoral; and they are gifted with beauty and musical powers not just because they really belong by birth to the urban upper class; they are also god-surrogates. The opera lover who has a taste for the fortunes of Pamino and Pamina in *The Magic Flute* is in the proper frame of mind for *Daphnis and Chloe*. (There are other attractive possibilities in this juxtaposition of Longus and Mozart, particularly the similarities one could develop in their rare mixture of erotic levity and syncretist religious gravity.)

What is the meaning and value of Longus' Arcadia? One might say that an Arcadia is just a species of the Golden Age (a "soft" primitivism as against a "hard"),[3] sharing in the virtues and vices of the latter's special reversed eschatology, and—like the Golden Age—a polar pair with the New Jerusalem and the coming Kingdom. But in fact there are various Arcadias with various significances. Sometimes the picture of Arcadia, the *ekphrasis*, is a genuine icon, or "artifice of eternity" (in Yeats's phrase).[4] One culmination of the pastoral and Arcadian tradition is Milton's Paradise:

> The birds their quire apply; airs, vernal airs,
> breathing the smell of field and grove, attune
> the trembling leaves, while universal Pan,
> knit with the Graces and the Hours in dance,
> led on th' eternal spring.
> *(Paradise Lost* IV 264–68)

In Milton's Paradise—and in Dante's Earthly Paradise also—transient nature is taken into the supernature where it is eternally preserved, a Resurrection of the World's Body.[5]

But Longus is not concerned with a world beyond the transient one. His icon of Arcadia shows forth his god, Eros, in the natural world, without intimations of a beyond. I should of course maintain that his icon, too, has revelatory power, but with a difference. The difference could be illustrated thus: most readers will be familiar with Plato's Myth of the Cave, wherein the life of unphilosophical darkness is represented. To emerge from the natural world into the awareness of the eternal, transcendent world is to pass from the cave into brilliant day.[6] Aristotle too had a Myth of the Cave:

> Suppose that there were men who had always lived under ground in good, bright homes adorned with statues and paintings, and that they had never gone above ground, but had learned by rumor and report that there was such a thing as divine power. Now suppose that at one time the jaws of earth opened and they could come out from their hidden abode into these regions where we dwell. When they had seen the unexpected sight of earth and seas and sky, had learned the grandeur of the clouds and might of winds . . . and when they beheld the entire heavens ranked and decked with stars . . . surely they would judge that gods too must exist, and that all this greatness was the work of gods. (Cicero, *On the Nature of the Gods* II 95)

Aristotle's Cave Myth is meant to suggest the glory of *this* world, and of the divinity as it is revealed in ordinary nature, not a transcendent super-nature. (The difference from Plato's Myth is characteristic of the general difference in the ontologies of the two philosophers.) Longus' myth, I would maintain, has a similar intent.

The temptation is great to indulge in comparisons with other poetic celebrations which are related in various ways to Longus. In two particularly intriguing cases I find the temptation irresistible.

> Summer, and noon, and a splendour of silence, felt,
> Seen, and heard of the spirit within the sense.
> . . . .
> I dare not sleep for delight of the perfect hour,
> Lest God be wroth that his gift should be scorned of
>   man.
> The face of the warm bright world is the face of a flower,
> The word of the wind and the leaves that the light
>   winds fan
> As the word that quickened at first into flame, and ran,

Creative and subtle and fierce with invasive power,
Through darkness and cloud, from the breath of the
    one God, Pan.

. . . .
But in all things evil and fearful that fear may scan,
As in all things good, as in all things fair that fall,
We know thee present and latent, the lord of man;
In the murmuring of doves, in the clamouring of winds
    that call
And wolves that howl for their prey; in the midnight's
    pall,
In the naked and nymph-like feet of the dawn, O Pan,
And in each life living, O thou the God who art all.
                  (Swinburne, "A Nympholept")

Swinburne is an unusually clear instance of the impact on a
post-Christian mind of precisely the pagan religious vision which
is found in *Daphnis and Chloe*. My second dithyrambist, however, is not so easily put in his place:

Nature and Man shall be disjoin'd and diffused no more,
The true son of God shall absolutely fuse them.

. . . .
Passage indeed O soul to primal thought,
Not lands and seas alone, thy own clear freshness,
The young maturity of brood and bloom,
To realms of budding bibles.

O soul, repressless, I with thee and thou with me,
Thy circumnavigation of the world begin,
Of man, the voyage of his mind's return,
To reason's early paradise,
Back, back to wisdom's birth, to innocent intuitions,
Again with fair creation.

. . . .
Passage to more than India!
O secret of the earth and sky!
Of you O waters of the sea! O winding creeks and rivers.
Of you O woods and fields! of you strong mountains of
    my land!
Of you O prairies! of you gray rocks!
O morning red! O clouds! O rain and snows!
O day and night, passage to you!
           (Whitman, "Passage to India")

My book should end here, but we are engaged in a critico-academic exercise, and topics remain. ("On," says Malone.) [7] Longus' program, explicit in his proem, is cure, comfort, and education through the *ekphrasis* of the immanent Eros. Of the importance of his program, and of his success in it, there will probably always be two minds, just as the whole of pagan antiquity will always have an ambivalent status for "the modern imagination"—at least in its Jewish and Christian form. On this question, and in a mood quite other than academic, I shall for the moment simply offer three different verdicts and leave the adjudication to the reader. The verdicts are all those of old men, and it is proper that this should be so, in a matter where youth is so easily led astray. The first is that of William Butler Yeats, whose "Sailing to Byzantium" I wilfully apply to our question:

> That is no country for old men. The young
> In one another's arms, birds in the trees
> —Those dying generations—at their song,
> The salmon-falls, the mackerel-crowded seas,
> Fish, flesh, or fowl, commend all summer long
> Whatever is begotten, born, and dies.
> Caught in that sensual music all neglect
> Monuments of unageing intellect.

The second is that of Mr. J. Littler, one of at least three previous owners of my copy of Mitscherlich's edition (1792) of the *Scriptores Erotici Graeci*. Mr. Littler apparently did not read the other Romances, but in June 1854, according to his marginal notations in an old man's script, he began *Daphnis and Chloe*, and finished it on February 19, 1855, although the previous day he had suffered from palpitations of the heart ("*aegrotans heri palpitatione cordis*"). His verdict:

. . . much more amusing than the metaphysics of the much bepraised Plato and Aristotle, which like pious drowsy sermons everyone (English) praises but nobody reads; which is more or less hypocrisy, at least one phase of the *crimen falsi*.

Johann Wolfgang Goethe in his eighty-first year (March 21, 1831) gave an evaluation of the work in his conversations with

Eckermann—an evaluation which is so famous and of such importance that it must be quoted at length:[8]

The work is so beautiful that, amid the wretched circumstances in which one lives, one cannot retain its effect, and one is always amazed anew when one rereads it. Sheer sunshine is in it, and one thinks he is seeing nothing but the wall-paintings of Herculaneum, while these pictures reciprocally influence the book by helping our imagination during the reading. . . . For all its restricted scope, it develops a complete world. . . . And the landscape, which a few decisive strokes so establish, that we see on the heights behind the persons vineyards, fields, and orchards, and down below, the pastures with the stream and a little woods, while in the distance are the reaches of the sea. . . .

The entire work manifests the highest art and culture. It is so thought out, that no theme is missing. . . . And a taste, a sensitive perfection of feeling, which is equal to the best elsewhere. All the disagreeable elements which disruptively intrude from outside upon the happy situations of the work, such as assault, kidnap, and war, are dismissed with utmost rapidity and leave hardly a trace behind. . . . In all this there is immense intelligence; also the preservation of Chloe's virginity through to the end of the novel, despite the aims of both lovers, who know no more than lying together naked—this also is superb, and so well motivated, that matters of greatest human import are given utterance. One would have to write an entire book to do justice to all its merits. It is well to read it once every year, to learn from it again and again, and to sense freshly its great beauty.

CHAPTER 9

Second Thoughts

THE discussion—or better, encomium—of *Daphnis and Chloe* in the preceding chapter was basically concerned with it as an Arcadian utopia. But there are a number of aspects of this particular Arcadia which are sufficiently wide-ranging to justify a separate chapter which will attempt to render a verdict on the work when it is judged in a larger context. These aspects I shall take up in the form of a series of provisional objections to its fundamentally Arcadian-utopian character: all of the objections question its "truth to life," its "relevance," or "significance."

In one sense, all of them may be dismissed as refusing to take the work on its own terms, within its own framework of expectation. But in another sense, it is in the long run impossible to treat literature as "pure" literature.[1] Every adequate interpretation and evaluation involves values and principles which are "extra-literary." Even the sheer choice to read or discuss *this* book ahead of *that* one cannot be separated from some form of basic decision which ramifies far beyond one's artificially delimited existence as book reader, beyond the cosmos of books into the wider cosmos which gives those books whatever power and significance they possess.

I *Nature*

In a work which so intently celebrates divine immanence in nature, invidious comparison with other works of comparable disposition is inevitable. The charge lies ready to hand: "This is no Nature; this is a prettified park, self-confessed. For the true Nature, one should turn to the nineteenth century (to Wordsworth, or, as the case may be, to Whitman, but their name is legion) or to the twentieth, where the true abysses, the otherness, and the intricate strangeness open up." All that Longus can man-

age, apparently, is to *list* the flowers; nothing at all like this
plunge into their intuited life:

> Flower-muscle, ever wider opening
> the meadow morning of anemone
> until the polyphonic light pours down
> loud from heaven into its lap . . .
>   (Rilke, *Sonnets to Orpheus* II 5)

Nor anything at all like Hopkins' "inscape":

The next morning a heavy fall of snow. It tufted and toed the firs and
yews and went on to load them till they were taxed beyond their
spring. The limes, elms, and Turkey-oaks it crisped beautifully as with
young leaf. Looking at the elms from underneath you saw every wave
in every twig (become by this the wire-like stem to a finger of snow)
and to the hangers and flying sprays it restored, to the eye, the in-
scapes they had lost. They were beautifully brought out against the
sky, which was on one side dead blue, on the other washed with
gold.[2]

The rejoinder is: Of course in Longus we are not given nature
"straight"; the delivery is deflected by the pastoral and other
artificial literary traditions, and the symbolic-religious (the
iconic) intent. It is something analogous to the "nature" of *The
Wind in the Willows* (with its epiphany of a benign, providential
Pan in "The Piper at the Gates of Dawn") or of the *Pastoral Symphony*, with serene brooks and birdsong, amusing rustic dances,
invigorating thunderstorms, and the shepherd's hymn of thanks-
giving.[3]

This utopian-pastoral deflection places the story of Daphnis and
Chloe next door to the fairy tale. All the same, are we justified
in saying that its "nature" is therefore less "real"? "Real" can
mean a variety of things, depending on a variety of possible
presuppositions. For example, one romantic conception of "real"
nature is that it is neither personal nor providential; its otherness
is nevertheless beneficent: it enables self-transcension and self-
loss, a merging into the World-all:

Thus I gave myself up more and more to blessed Nature, and almost
too unreservedly. How gladly I would have become a child, to be

closer to her; how gladly I would have known less and become like
the pure beam of light, to be closer to her! To feel myself for a
moment in her peace, her beauty—how much more that meant to me
than years of thought, than all the efforts of endlessly effortful men.
(Hölderlin, *Hyperion*, final letter)

But a more hardheaded or cold-blooded doctrine (existentialist,
let us say) would check all glorious mystical plunges by proclaim-
ing the absurdity of nature, the utter immiscibility between the
natural and *any* human meaning—including that of ecstatic self-
loss. Or again, from the opposite side, one could affirm the fundamentally personal character of the life of nature; this was the
affirmation made in various ways by much of pagan antiquity.
(Cf. ". . . And the azurous hung hills are his world-wielding
shoulder," Hopkins, "Hurrahing in Harvest.")

My claim would therefore be that *every* literary stance toward
"nature" (including even the sheer demarcation of "nature" as a
separate literary subject) will be found to deflect and distort the
"reality" in the direction hiddenly imposed not only by its literary-
stylistic tradition, but also by its implicit metaphysics. Insofar as
literature serves as an attempt to name the nameless, it imposes
a mythical (i.e., metaphysical) distortion derived from the un-
avoidably specific form of the "name" (i.e., of the mythical structure) which it employs. (This view is related to a general view of
language as interacting with the "reality" it is supposed to
serve.) [4] Yet, as language in general is necessary and good, so
literature in its attempts to name—otherwise the earth would be
"without form, and void."

It is therefore possible to espouse the "reality" of Longus' per-
sonalized "nature"; it is at least one valid option among a number
of possible realities.

II *Stylistic Artifice*

Longus has also been attacked for the unreality of his style.
Of his language it is said that it is unsuited to true pastoral plain-
ness and directness. This recalls the old manifesto of Wordsworth
on behalf of "the language really used by men" in poetry.[5] Coleridge's rejoinder in *Biographia Literaria* applies in principle as
well against the stylistic detractors of Longus as it originally did
against Wordsworth himself:

The best part of human language, properly so called, is derived from
reflection on the acts of the mind itself. It is formed by a voluntary
appropriation of fixed symbols to internal acts, to processes and results of imagination, the greater part of which have no place in the
consciousness of uneducated men.[6]

In Longus' case, to be sure, it is not so much the intellectual diction as it is the intellectual rhetoric, the word craft, which is
"false" to the rustic subject. But the art is directed at evoking a
complex, quasi-musical response from highly educated readers
who are sensitive to such form, and the gain in esthetic richness
is comparable to that which Coleridge claimed for the use of educated language. The linguistic artifice enables a more complex
presentation of the total experience than "natural" speech would.
The outlandishness of Gerard Manley Hopkins is in fact further
inland than Wordsworth.

III *Utopian Optimism*

Longus can also be charged with unreality in his fundamentally unproblematic, providentially optimistic treatment of man at
home in the divine-natural life, with a happy ending. On this, let
me quote a recent defense of some kinds of unreal stories:

The peculiar quality of the "joy" in successful Fantasy can thus be
explained as a sudden glimpse of the underlying reality or truth. It
is not only a "consolation" for the sorrow of this world, but a satis-
faction, and an answer to that question, "Is it true?" The answer to
this question that I gave at first was (quite rightly): "If you have
built your little world well, yes: it is true in that world." That is
enough for the artist (or the artist part of the artist). But in the "euca-
tastrophe" we see in a brief vision that the answer may be greater—it
may be a far-off gleam or echo of *evangelium* in the real world. . . .
All tales may come true; and yet, at the last, redeemed, they may be
as like and as unlike the forms that we give them as Man, finally
redeemed, will be like and unlike the fallen that we know.[7]

Tolkien's remarks on "happy endings" apply with particular
directness to some works which relate immediately to Longus:
A Winter's Tale and *The Tempest*. (Recent work supports the
probability that *Daphnis and Chloe* directly influenced *The*

Tempest;[8] its influence, direct and indirect, on *A Winter's Tale* is already well known.)[9] But in these there is a conscious adumbration of Christian and otherworldly themes, of the sort for which Tolkien suggests that the fairy story provides an unconscious adumbration. (Consider, for example, the Resurrection in "The Sleeping Beauty.") Longus' tale, on the other hand, belongs deliberately to this world only. But no matter how much he (and more recent pagans) may protest, the wisdom of Christianity has seen a way to include such terrene evocations as a *part* of the truth, even if not the whole truth. And the resurrected body cannot but rediscover in eternal life, in the "restitution of all things," its immemorial companion, the physical world.[10] For the Christian, the final form of the Romance may be Dante's reunion with Beatrice in the Earthly Paradise. From this viewpoint, then, Longus utopian praise of Erotic nature willy-nilly finds its validation.

IV *Cynicism*

But what really threatens to tumble the whole dream house—and what fatally vitiated *Daphnis and Chloe* for such people as Rohde—is the fact that Longus refuses to be serious about his own "message": he readily undercuts it at various points with foolery, irony, mockery, and lubricity.

One may grant validity to the treatment of the love of this youthful herdsman-pair as something hardly more than a sweet sensual desire. But the way in which the author whips up this desire and, through lascivious experimentation, keeps on bringing it to a point just short of gratification—this betrays a revolting, hypocritical sophistication and makes us most unpleasantly aware that all the naïveté of this idyllist is only an artificial concoction, and that he himself is in fact nothing more than a *Sophist*.[11]

Thus Rohde. Here, however, is where the twentieth century is better equipped to read Longus than the nineteenth. Cultivation of ambivalence, cloaking serious in jest, mixing passion and titters —these are not so hard to accept now, though every worthy listener to Mozart should have been in possession of the secret even before the nineteenth century. H. O. Chalk has the right word here:

It is this sophisticated irony which saves Longus from the insipidity of countless later pastorals. It also saves him from the tedium which the ponderous mumbo-jumbo of his Erotic mystery might easily have induced: when he is at his most serious he is simultaneously at his most cynically witty.[12]

Precisely this ambivalence floats *Daphnis and Chloe* lightly past all the backwaters in which many a sober and improving moral tale is now lodged—say, *Rasselas,* or that closest emulation of Longus, Bernardin de Saint-Pierre's *Paul and Virginia.*[13] The case is adjunct to *Lolita.*[14]

V   *Contemporary Irrelevance*

Is there any way in which our own living has any direct relation to the ideal vision presented in Longus? I do not wish to pontificate as mandarin spokesman for an age; the question is simply whether anything is at stake in *Daphnis and Chloe* which is worth the attention of other than the historical dilettante (which the classicist as "professional" often amounts to). There are several ways in which an affirmative claim could be made.

In the first place, *Daphnis and Chloe* holds up an image of primal health, a state in which the civilized dissociation from nature and the divinity which sustains it is overcome. As Jack Lindsay says,

He turns to the poetic tradition and sifts it through for the imagery of love and happiness, for the dream of a rich and innocent earth in which all the problems of history are lyrically resolved or forgotten.[15]

Probably the best current indication of the vitality of this ideal can be found in two books by Norman O. Brown: *Life Against Death,* and *Love's Body.*[16] (Something of the polysemantic omnireferent use of imagery by Brown can be seen in Longus as well.) Brown's modern syncretism is much more radical and mantic, but the points of contact are many, including that abolition of history which Lindsay remarked in Longus:

Man, the discontented animal, unconsciously seeking the life proper to his species, is man in history: repression and the repetition-compulsion generate historical time. . . . And conversely, life not repressed—organic life below man and human life if repression were overcome—is not in historical time.[17]

Very good, one may say, but the pastorality of the book effectively closes it off from us. The resurrected body as preached by Norman Brown does not require flocks of sheep, gardens, and running brooks for its realization. Further, the social-psychological future of mankind is in the cities: utopia will have to be conceived in urban form.

To this the reply could run: despite critiques of village and pastoral life—such as that in Harvey Cox's *The Secular City*[18]— the pastorality of *Daphnis and Chloe* is one of the most important and crucial things about it; the book keeps alive the ideal of pasture and park. For what our cities need, among other things, is an infusion of countryside: the urban aggregate is, or soon will be, technologically out of date. Lewis Mumford:

When I ask myself what immediate improvement would make my own city, New York, more attractive to live in again, I find two answers: rows of shade trees on every street, and a little park, even a quarter of an acre, in each block, preferably near the middle.[19]

When the park-and-pasture city is at last technologically achieved, this perennial problem child of civilization (a problem ever since Jericho, or even since Enoch, the city of shepherd-hating Cain in the Land of Nod) will finally have started to learn how to behave.[20]

But in fact the city can only really be healed if the society which concentrates in it is also healed (I write this in the summer of the Newark and Detroit riots). And—all things considered—Longus has some remarkable emphases in this direction. To be sure, as Lindsay says, "the problems of history are lyrically resolved or forgotten," but look at the form taken by that lyric: Lindsay is also the only student who notes that, while the other Romances have a "middle class coloration" (lovers and their families explicitly belonging to that class or higher), *Daphnis and Chloe* gives central and affectionate interest to peasants and herdsmen.[21] (Mao Tse-Tung reports that, while eagerly devouring the old Chinese romances when he was a boy, "It occurred

to me one day that there was one thing peculiar about these
stories and that was the absence of peasants who tilled the
land.") [22]

But even this interest could be nearly paralleled by cases in
New Comedy. The really striking thing is that these peasant
herdsmen are *slaves*. I can think of no other work of ancient
literature where the hero and heroine are slaves from birth. (New
Comedy, Roman Comedy, and Euripides make some approaches,
but do not go this far. Enslavement is one of the standard mis-
haps in Romance, and the pathos of bondage is frequently exploited, but it is a transitory, not fundamental, condition.) To
be sure, the work hedges the class issue by emphasizing that
Daphnis and Chloe are obviously superior to their apparent
birth; but the seriousness of their slave status is emphasized in
such things as their fearful anticipation of Dionysophanes' arrival
and in Daphnis' outrageous helplessness as chattel which could
have been handed over as a plaything to the debauched Gnathon.
And Daphnis, but for Providence, would probably have had to
renounce Chloe as beneath his station. So the restoration of them
and their foster parents to freedom at the end does effect a kind
of lyric overleaping, or resolution, of the social cleft, especially
since these newly established members of the upper-class gentry
choose to remain in the country and live as rustics for the rest of
their lives.

VI *Absence of Historical Dialectic*

The fundamental lack in Longus (the only important one to
my mind, though one should not perhaps expect everything from
every author) is not the elements missing from his utopia. Rather,
it is the sheer fact of its utopianism. Despite everything said so
far, there remain irremediably problematic aspects to any utopian
literature—even more when the utopia is Arcadian. The topic is
so immense and many-sided that I am incapable of coping with
it as it deserves (see Ernst Bloch's *Das Prinzip Hoffnung*). I
shall here approach it from only one side, as it seems to open
itself to me.

A utopian work makes a claim, by definition, to be showing
society ideally ordered. But if the ideal picture of that society
lacks penetration into the real detail of any social structure, the
order will be superficial and its contemplation fruitless, except

perhaps for escapism and lollipop-sucking. For a detailed picture, the historical and social forces of our actual imperfect society must, in some transformed way, be incorporated. Only then does our present have a real—a dialectical—connection with that ideal future. "The tendencies leading to the future are in fact more firmly and definitely contained in what really is than in the most beautiful utopian dreams or projections." [23] But Longus has no such grounding in history and its grim forward-backward, round-about social clashes. (Not all the ancient pagans—Vergil and Aeschylus prove it—lacked a sense for historical process.)

Furthermore, the pastoral-Arcadian element in Longus' utopia involves an additional claim: to show human nature integrated into the erotic-natural cosmos. Once again, the endlessly subtle character of our moral-psychological present existence must form part of that picture of integration, though it may suffer sea-change before it gets there. If Longus were actually to have faced the problem, he would in fact have been driven far beyond his mannerist naturalism to some equivalent of the *Divine Comedy*, wherein the love which rules the cosmos is approached more nearly. As it is, his vision does not gather up the actual moral and psychological complexity of human motive and action.

So Longus gives us no inkling of how we can get from *here* (e.g., from suppurating cities and psyches and class strife) to *there;* he merely says "Eros will find a way." Putting it differently: his absorption in nature and its rhythms prevents his awareness of the crucial difference of man from nature, the difference which generates history and freedom.[24]

It is only in the past century that the constraints and dilemmas involved in the historicity of personhood have been faced, accepted, and incorporated into a utopian vision in such a way as actually to mark out a path (even though of the utmost provisionality) toward that utopia, whose central features are: (1) a restored unity-in-cooperation with our natural environment as a corporate policy of the entire society;[25] and (2) the overcoming of class strife within the society via the elevation of its productive workers to power and the elimination of private capital. ("Productive workers" is of course a phrase requiring much analysis and qualification. In the simple agrarian economy of *Daphnis and Chloe* it would apply to the peasant-slaves.) In the words of one such utopian path-marker:

It is essential to unite with the middle peasants, and it is wrong not
to do so. But on whom must the workingclass and the Communist
Party rely in the countryside in order to unite with the middle peasants and realize the socialist transformation of the entire countryside?
Surely on none other than the poor peasants. That was the case when
the struggle against the landlords was being waged and the land reform was being carried out, and that is the case today when the
struggle against the rich peasants and other capitalist elements is
being waged to achieve the socialist transformation of agriculture.
. . . The poor peasant must work on the middle peasants and win
them over, so that the revolution will broaden from day to day until
final victory.[26]

To make the point in a broad and sweeping symbolic way:
the peasant-poet-revolutionary Mao Tse-Tung (or any equivalent
agrarian revolutionary) is the final form of the pastoral artist
when the Arcadian vision is seriously mapped out in terms of
cold, appalling, historical-political necessity.

The emergence of Longus' natural Eros in this, its deepest,
most historically embedded communal form (or rather, its re-
surgence in the realm of technological civilization, after ages of
banishment, from the time of the large-scale dissolution of primitive tribes)—this emergence is of course gravely threatened, both
by internal contradictions and by external conflict. The specula-
tive observer is tempted to employ Freud's mythology of the
eternal struggle between Eros and Thanatos, and he is inclined
to fear that Thanatos may be having its innings for the rest of
this century, if not forever.[27]

The relationship between a work of narrative literature and
this struggle can vary endlessly. But the worth of the literature
is likely to depend partly on the degree to which it is sensitive
to the qualities of actual (historically situated) life as it is involved in this struggle. From this point of view *Daphnis and
Chloe* is two-dimensional and static.[28]

Whatever its shortcomings, *Daphnis and Chloe* is at least
clearly on the side of Eros and Flower-power against the Bomb
and Thanatos. If Longus had lived at the *fin de siècle,* one can
imagine him, along with Ruskin, Morris, and Wilde, as a genteel
esthetic socialist.[29] On the level of its actual impact on lived life,
our final verdict on *Daphnis and Chloe* should depend on whether

we can say that this utopian, this hippie icon ultimately serves to reinforce the movement of historical Eros—whether it really (like the winter *Dionysia* in Dryas' cottage) helps evoke the returning powers of spring, lest Pan die.

Notes and References

Preface

1. For example: A. Chassang, *Histoire du roman . . . dans l'anti-quité grecque et latine* (Paris, 1862); J. Ludvíkovsky, *Recky Roman Dobrodružny* (Prague, 1925); R. Merkelbach, *Roman und Mysterium in der Antike* (München-Berlin, 1962); O. Schissel von Fleschenberg, *Entwicklungsgeschichte des griechischen Romanes im Altertum* (Halle, 1913); E. E. Seiler, *Longi Pastoralia* (Leipzig, 1843); and a number of articles.

2. The works of Braun, Kerènyi, Lavagnini, Mittelstadt, Georg Rohde, and Schwartz (see Bibliography). Ernst Bloch's remarkable work *Das Prinzip Hoffnung* (Frankfurt am Main, 1959) came to my attention too late to be of use in the shaping of my speculative-theoretical remarks in the last two chapters.

3. Thus in the editions of Dalmeyda (Longus, *Pastorales*, ed. Georges Dalmeyda, 2d ed., Paris, 1960) and Schönberger (Longus, *Hirtengeschichten von Daphnis und Chloe*, ed. Otto Schönberger, Berlin, 1960). Another version would (in English) add "Lesbian" before "Pastoral," as in Edmonds' edition (Longus, *Daphnis and Chloe*, trans. George Thornley, ed. J. M. Edmonds, London, 1916).

Chronology

1. Schönberger (above, Preface, n. 3), pp. 1–3.

Chapter One

1. I am obliged to several members of the Department of English at Kenyon College for the reference to Milton.

2. See Chronology. I owe the suggestion of a connection between Longus and the passage in Plutarch to Aristide Calderini in "Prolegomeni, V," Caritone di Afrodisia, *Le avventure di Cherea e Callirhoe*, trans. Aristide Calderini (Turin, 1913).

3. Longus has here appropriated motifs which first appear in the *Homeric Hymn to Dionysos*: the god, appearing as a youth along the sea-shore, is kidnapped by pirates. Suddenly a vine spreads out at the top of the sail, and ivy curls around the mast; there are wreaths on

the oar-locks. Dionysos turns into a lion. The sailors panic, jump overboard, and turn into dolphins. (Ezra Pound has developed this material in the second of his *Cantos*.) For the significance of Longus' use
of this *Homeric Hymn*, see Chapter 6.

4. Stephen Leacock, "Homer and Humbug, an Academic Discussion," *Behind the Beyond, and Other Contributions to Human Knowledge* (New York: John Lane, 1921) reprinted in *Arion* II 4 (Winter
1963), 85.

5. The date of the story is merely implicit. To some degree it is misleading to speak of any specific temporal setting for this utopian narrative.

6. I bypass, as a topic for estheticians, the question how far "misun-
derstanding" and "understanding" are systematic in all artistic experience.

7. Johann Peter Eckermann, "Sonntag, den 20 März 1831," *Ge-
spräche mit Goethe*, in Johann Wolfgang Goethe, *Gedenkausgabe der
Werke, Briefe, und Gespräche* (Zürich: Artemis, 1948), XXIV, 484.
See the extensive quotation from this passage in Chapter 8, p. 106.

Chapter Two

1. For Xenophon of Ephesos, Achilleus Tatios, and Heliodoros I
follow the dating suggested in Otto Weinreich, *Der griechische Liebesroman* (Zürich: Artemis, 1962), pp. 10–21. For *The Life of Apollonios
of Tyre*, see Ben Edwin Perry, *The Ancient Romances: A Literary-
Historical Account of Their Origins* (Berkeley and Los Angeles: University of California, 1967), p. 294.

2. First published 1876. Fourth edition, Hildesheim: Georg Olms,
1960.

3. Sophie Trenkner, *The Greek Novella in The Classical Period*
(Cambridge, Eng.: Cambridge University, 1958).

4. Above, n. 1.

5. Perry, pp. 8–15 and *passim*.

6. Trenkner, p. 77.

7. Sophocles' *Phaidra* (now lost) probably pointed the way for
Euripides.

8. Diodoros of Sicily II 50ff.

9. Plato: for example, *The Republic*, or *Timaios* 23–25 and *Kritias;*
Homer: *Odyssey* VI–VIII.

10. Perry, pp. 45–46 and Chapter II *passim*.

11. See especially "Fortunata," *Mimesis: The Representation of Reality in Western Literature*, trans. Willard Trask (Princeton: Princeton
University, 1953). A more specialized treatment is given by Auerbach
later in "*Sermo Humilis*," *Literary Language and Its Public in Late*

Latin Antiquity and in the Middle Ages, trans. Ralph Manheim (New York: Bollingen Foundation, 1965).

12. Perry, pp. 138–39.

13. Gunnar Valley, *Über den Sprachgebrauch des Longus* (Uppsala: Berling, 1926), p. 102, notes that this connection was made by Boissonade (no reference given). It is also made by Paul Turner, "Daphnis and Chloe: An Interpretation," *Greece and Rome,* 2d Ser., VII (1960), 117. I am intrigued by another possible echo: Plutarch says that Isis recorded her sufferings and achievements "both as a lesson in piety and a consolation for men and women subjected to similar misfortunes." (*On Isis and Osiris* 27.)

14. Jack Lindsay, critical essay appended to Longus, *Daphnis and Chloe,* trans. Jack Lindsay (London: Daimon, 1948), pp. 97–103; H. H. O. Chalk, "Eros and the Lesbian Pastorals of Longos," *Journal of Hellenic Studies,* LXXX (1960), 44–47.

Chapter Three

1. For Lyly's sources and influence there is a full discussion by R. Warwick Bond in "Essay on Euphues and Euphuism," *The Complete Works of John Lyly,* ed. R. Warwick Bond (Oxford: Clarendon Press, 1902), Vol. I.

2. Full treatment of the Second Sophistic in Eduard Norden, *Die antike Kunstprosa vom VI. Jahrhundert v. Chr. bis in die Zeit der Renaissance,* 5th ed. (Stuttgart: Teubner, 1958), Vol. I, and in Wilhelm Schmid and Otto Stählin, *Wilhelm von Christ's Geschichte der griechischen Literatur,* 6th ed., Part II, second half (Munich: Beck, 1924).

3. Rohde, pp. 550–54.

4. Samuel Lee Wolff, *The Greek Romances in Elizabethan Prose Fiction* (New York: Columbia University, 1912), pp. 234–35.

5. J. Maillon, "Preface du traducteur," in Héliodore, *Les Éthiopiques,* ed. R. M. Rattenbury and T. W. Lumb, trans. J. Maillon, 2d ed. (Paris: Les Belles Lettres, 1960), I, xciii. This could also be said of Faulkner's baroque, at least in the bad moments.

6. Valley, "Vorwort," p. iii.

7. E.g., III 23 *melê:* limbs/songs; II 15 *aigas:* goats/waves.

8. Rohde, pp. 550–54.

9. Introduction, Petronius, *The Satyricon,* trans. William Arrowsmith (New York: New American Library, 1960), p. xi.

10. W. B. Stanford, *The Sound of Greek* (Berkeley and Los Angeles: University of California, 1967), pp. 1–3.

11. Edward Gibbon, *The Decline and Fall of the Roman Empire,* Chapter III (Vol. I, p. 70 in the Modern Library edition).

12. William K. Prentice, Introduction, Dion Chrysostom, *The Hunt-*

ers of Euboea, ed. William K. Prentice (Boston: Allyn and Bacon, 1897), p. vi. Rostovtzeff accounts for the economic change thus: "[In the developing Roman empire] districts which had formerly depended upon imports from the large manufacturing centres now began to take a share in production. Hence, the large centres lost their economic position and grew impoverished. The worst plight of all was that of Greece, whose manufactures disappeared almost entirely from the world's market." M. Rostovtzeff, *Rome,* trans. J. D. Duff, Galaxy Book edn. by Elias J. Bickerman (New York: Oxford University, 1960; first published as Vol. II of *A History of the Ancient World,* 1927), p. 259.

13. On infanticide among the Greeks, see W. W. Tarn, *Hellenistic Civilisation,* 3d ed. (Cleveland and New York: World, 1961), pp. 100–102, to whom I owe the reference to Poseidippos, the comic poet quoted in the text (Poseidippos No. 11, Edmonds, *The Fragments of Attic Comedy*).

Chapter Four

1. J. Huizinga, *The Waning of the Middle Ages* (New York: Doubleday and Company, n.d.; first published in English, 1924), p. 134. I owe this reference to Chalk, p. 48.

2. Gilbert Lawall, *Theocritus' Coan Pastorals: A Poetry Book* (Cambridge, Mass.: Harvard University, 1967). Lawall shows that even what I call the "simple" pastorals reveal unsuspected layers when attention is given to their elliptical treatment of certain themes.

3. For the first two examples, see *Select Papyri,* Vol. III: *Literary Papyri: Poetry,* ed. D. L. Page, 2d ed. (Cambridge, Mass.: Harvard University, 1942), nos. 77 and 79. For the third: Herondas (Herodes), *Mimiambi* III.

4. B. A. van Groningen makes this association from another direction in *"La poésie verbale Grecque: essai de mise au point," Mededelingen der Koninklijke Nederlandse Akademie van Wetenschappen, Afd. Letterkunde* (Amsterdam, 1953). Reference in Perry, pp. 179 and 360.

5. Lawall, Chapter VII.

6. Bruno Snell, "Arcadia: The Discovery of a Spiritual Landscape," *The Discovery of the Mind: The Greek Origins of European Thought,* trans. T. G. Rosenmeyer (Cambridge, Mass.: Harvard University, 1953).

Chapter Five

1. See, for example, Introduction, in Dalmeyda's edition of Longus (above, Preface, n. 3), pp. xviii–xx and *The Letters of Alciphron, Aelian, and Philostratus,* ed. Allen Rogers Benner and Francis H. Fobes (Cambridge, Mass.: Harvard University, 1959), p. 18.

2. Hermogenes, *On Forms* II 4 (*Rhetores Graeci,* ed. Leonard Spengel, Leipzig: Teubner, 1856, II, 357–64); Demetrius, *On Style* III 132, 163 (in Aristotle, *The Poetics,* ed. W. Hamilton Fyfe, etc., 2d ed. [Cambridge, Mass.: Harvard University, 1932]). I owe the original references to Schönberger, p. 23.

3. Oscar Wilde, "The Selfish Giant," *Fairy Tales,* in *The Writings of Oscar Wilde* (New York: Wm. H. Wise, 1931), II, 38–39.

4. For one rather close approach, consider this from "The Fisherman and His Soul," Wilde (above, n. 3), p. 164: "Her hair was as a wet fleece of gold, and each separate hair as a thread of fine gold in a cup of glass. Her body was as white ivory, and her tail was of silver and pearl. Silver and pearl was her tail, and the green weeds of the sea coiled round it; and like sea-shells were her ears, and her lips were like sea-coral. The cold waves dashed over her cold breasts, and the salt glistened upon her eyelids."

5. Lyly, ed. Bond (above, Chapter 3, n. 1), I, 202. For a full analysis of Lyly's style, along with many illustrations, see Bond's introduction, pp. 120ff.

6. J. B. C. d'Ansse de Villoison, quoted (presumably from his 1778 edition of Longus, which I have not seen) by P. Petit-Radel, "Proasma," *Longi Sophistae Pastoralia Lesbiaca . . . Poema Erotico-Poimenicon e textu Graeco in Latinum numeris heroicis deductum* (Paris, 1809), pp. xxvii–xxviii.

7. See, for example, William Arrowsmith and Roger Shattuck, eds., *The Craft and Context of Translation: A Critical Symposium* (New York: Doubleday and Company, 1964), and D. S. Carne-Ross, "Postscript" to Homer, *Patrocleia,* trans. Christopher Logue (Ann Arbor: University of Michigan, 1963).

8. "The effect of studying masterpieces is to make me admire and do otherwise." Gerard Manley Hopkins, letter to Robert Bridges, Sept. 25, 1888, in *Poems and Prose of Gerard Manley Hopkins,* ed. W. H. Gardner (London: Penguin Books, 1953), p. 207.

9. *Three Greek Romances,* trans. Moses Hadas (New York: Doubleday and Company, 1953), pp. 21–22.

10. *Daphnis and Chloe: A Most Sweet and Pleasant Pastoral Romance for Young Ladies,* trans. George Thornley. First published London, 1657; the quotation may be found in the reprint by Pantheon Books, 1949, on pp. 25–26, and in the revised, bowdlerized edition by Edmonds (above, Preface, n. 3) on pp. 21 and 23. Some readers may wish to compare Amyot:

oyans chanter les oyseaux, ilz chantoyent; voyant saulter les aigneaux, ilz saultoient; et, comme les abeilles, alloyent cueillans des fleurs. . . . Leurs jeux estoyent jeux de bergers et d'enfans: car elle alloit quelque part cueillir des joncs, dont elle faisoit un cofin à mettre des cigales, et ce pendant ne se soucyoit aucunement de son troupeau; luy, d'autre costé, alloit coupper des rouseaux, et en pertuisoit les joinctures, puis les recolloit ensemble avec de la cyre molle, et aprenoit à en jouer, bien souvent jusques à la nuict.

Further comparative samples:

In so much as with the birds they sang, seing the kids leape, they daunced, and after the bees they gathered flowers. . . . Their exercises were in Sheapehearde games, and the pleasures they intertained, such as beseemed the nonage of their outgrowing childhood, for some part of their time, they spent in gathering bulrushes, wherewith Chloe would make pretie bird cages and therein put the grasshoppers. Daphnis on the other side often times cut downe the reedes, and unclosing their ioints, glewed them orderlie together againe with soft waxe, and of these found divers pastimes wherewith to occupie them selves togethers. (Angel Day)

For hearing the birds sing, they sang; seeing the lambs skip, they skipped; and then like the bees they sought flowers. . . . Sometimes one kept watch over the two flocks whilst the other engaged in some prank, the pranks of shepherds and of children. Scampering forth in the morning she would gather some rushes to make a cage for a grasshopper, and so wholly bent was she on the weaving that her flock was forgotten. At a little distance Daphnis cut reeds, and after cleaning away the joints and joining the reeds together with soft wax, he practised playing the double flute all day till nightfall. (George Moore, *The Pastoral Loves of Daphnis and Chloe,* New York: Limited Editions Club, 1934, p. 5)

They heard the birds sing; so they sang. They saw the lambs skipping; so they leaped nimbly. They vied with the bees in culling flowers. . . . All their toys were those of shepherds or of children. Chloe, scampering hither and thither, would find out windlestraws and weave a grasshopper cage; and, working intently, she would neglect her sheep. Daphnis had cut some slender reeds, bored through the partitions at the joints, and fitted them together with soft wax; and now he cared only for piping till dusk came. (Jack Lindsay, *Daphnis and Chloe,* London: Daimon, 1948, p. 7)

11. Longus, *Daphnis and Chloe,* trans. Paul Turner (London: Penguin Books, 1956), pp. 23–24.

12. Jack Lindsay's translation, within the limits of its conventional fidelity to the text, is excellent and should be reprinted in paperback.

13. Modified from the structure given by Schönberger, p. 25.

Among the aspects of Longus' art which I have not recapitulated in the text is his organization of the plot—above and beyond its amoebeism—into a repeated tripartite sequence of which the following from the opening of Book I is a sample:

(1) Description of the setting;
(2) (a) Discovery of Daphnis;
     (b) Discovery of Chloe;
(3) The two herd their flocks together.

The sequence regularly involves descriptive setting, two actions separately concerning Daphnis and Chloe, and their reunion in an idyllic tableau with an enhanced emotional-psychological tone. This organization was pointed out by Schissel von Fleschenberg (reference in Schönberger, p. 25). It has recently been strikingly illuminated by Mittelstadt in connection with the technique of narrative landscape painting which flourished contemporary with Longus (for example, the "Odyssey-landscapes"). See Michael Charles Mittelstadt, "Longus and the Greek Love Romance" (Dissertation, Stanford University, 1964: University Microfilms), pp. 120ff.

14. See, for example, George E. Duckworth, *Structural Patterns and Proportions in Vergil's Aeneid* (Ann Arbor: University of Michigan, 1962).

15. Schönberger, pp. 161–62; Chalk, pp. 40–42. I have detailed the connections of these stories with their context at greater length than either of the above.

16. See Chapter 6, and Chalk pp. 34–35 for the assimilation of Eros and Dionysos.

17. Valley, p. 79.

18. For a full and careful examination of other ways in which bucolic poetry is adapted by Longus, see Georg Rohde, "Longus und die Bukolik," *Rheinisches Museum,* 86 (1937), 23–49.

19. Chalk, pp. 46–47.

20. The bee had a variety of religious connotations. See Jane Harrison, *Prolegomena to the Study of Greek Religion* (New York: Meridian Books, 1955; reprint of 3d ed., 1922), pp. 442–43. In Vergil's *Georgics* IV they are treated as symbols of immortality and regeneration.

Chapter Six

1. Albin Lesky, *Geschichte der griechischen Literatur,* 2d ed. (Bern and Munich: Francke, 1963), p. 917.

2. Auerbach (above, Chapter 2, n. 11), Chapter 3.

3. Auerbach, pp. 18–19, 35–43, and *passim.*

4. The pseudonymity is supported by Schmid-Stählin (above, Chapter 3, n. 2), p. 368.

5. T. R. Glover, *Conflict of Religions in the Early Roman Empire,* 3d ed. (London: Methuen, 1910), p. 111, quoted in Chalk, p. 44.

6. Dylan Thomas, *Collected Poems 1934–1952* (London: J. M. Dent and Sons, 1952), p. 9.

7. Lindsay, pp. 103–4.

8. Liddell-Scott-Jones, *A Greek-English Lexicon* (Oxford, 1940), s.v.

9. Chalk, p. 38.

10. Chalk, p. 43, and W. K. C. Guthrie, *Orpheus and Greek Religion: A Study of the Orphic Movement* (reprint New York: W. W. Norton and Company, 1966), pp. 95ff.

11. Chalk, p. 48, n. 107, with Merkelbach (below, n. 16), p. 47.

12. Chalk, pp. 36–39.

13. Compare an epigram by Anyte—who was probably influential upon Longus (Schönberger, p. 11):

—Why, rustic Pan, do you sit alone in the shadowy wood
      and play on your sweet-voiced pipes?
—So my cattle may graze over these dew-fresh hills,
      culling the field's fair leafage.
      (Anyte XIX Gow-Page/*Greek Anthology* I 231)

14. See Chapter 1, n. 3.

15. E.g., I 27 and II 7.

16. The major works of this school: K. Kerenyi, *Die griechisch-orientalische Romanliteratur in religionsgeschichtlicher Beleuchtung* (Tübingen: Mohr, 1927); R. Merkelbach, *Roman und Mysterium in der Antike* (Munich-Berlin, 1962). Of Merkelbach I have seen only his earlier article, concerned with *Daphnis and Chloe* alone: "*Daphnis und Chloe: Roman und Mysterium,*" *Antaios* I (1960), 47–60.

17. Chalk, pp. 42–45.

18. Compare Vergil, *Georgics* IV 557–58, where the regenerated bees are described as hanging from a tree in a swarm like a grape cluster.

Chapter Seven

1. Cf. Agamemnon's dream in *Iliad* II, and those of Croesus and Xerxes in Herodotos (I 34; VII 12ff.).

2. Arion, a dithyrambic (Dionysian) poet is rescued from robber sailors and rides safe to shore on a dolphin in Herodotos I 23–24; compare also the capture of Dionysos as a youth on the shore by pirates and his escape in the *Homeric Hymn to Dionysos* (above, Chapter 1, n. 3); see further connections with Dionysos in Chalk, p. 46, n. 99.

3. Once more, the *Hymn to Dionysos* (above, n. 2).

4. Xenophon's party is climaxed with a mimic enactment of an erotic myth (*Symposium* IX).

5. Compare Vergil, *Eclogues* II 36–38; V 85–87.
6. Chalk, pp. 46–47.
7. Pseudo-Aristotle, *On the Cosmos* 401ª 15: "He [Zeus] is called the son of Kronos and of Chronos."
8. p. 14.
9. See, for example, fr. 167 in Otto Kern, *Orphicorum Fragmenta* (Berlin: Weidmann, 1922), p. 200.

Chapter Eight

1. This statement does not apply to Daphnis in I and Lycidas in VII, who are in a class apart from ordinary herdsmen. Even among the latter there may exist a condition of ideal equity and amiability, as in VI (see Lawall, Chapter VI), and to this extent my metaphor of the hybrid is not perfectly apt.
2. For Snell, see above, Chapter 4, n. 6.
3. These terms are borrowed from their use in Erwin Panofsky, "*Et in Arcadia Ego:* Poussin and the Elegiac Tradition," *Meaning in the Visual Arts* (New York: Doubleday and Company, 1957), p. 297.
4. "Sailing to Byzantium," III. For some forms of Arcadia in actual painting, see, in addition to Panofsky (above, n. 3), Kenneth Clark, "Ideal Landscape," *Landscape into Art* (Boston: Beacon Press, 1961; first published 1949).
5. For another sort of Arcadian culmination, see Marvell's "The Garden," together with the discussion by William Empson in Chapter IV of *Some Versions of Pastoral* (Norfolk, Conn.: New Directions, 1960, first published London, 1936).
6. *Republic* VII 514ª–521ᵇ.
7. Samuel Beckett, *Malone Dies* (New York: Grove Press, 1956), p. 111. I am indebted for this reference to Professor John E. Maher.
8. Goethe's enthusiasm has been explained away variously—by Rohde, for example (p. 549, n. 3), on the grounds that Goethe knew only a French translation superior to the original. Schönberger seems to me (pp. 20–22) successfully to vindicate the validity of Goethe's remarks as a judgment on the Greek original. Eckermann himself makes a comparison of Goethe and Longus in "Dienstag, den 15. März 1831." For a different version of the refreshing power of *Daphnis and Chloe* as felt by an old man, compare George Moore's introduction to his translation.

Chapter Nine

1. For a very persuasive argument to the contrary, see Northrop Frye, "Polemical Introduction," *Anatomy of Criticism: Four Essays* (Princeton: Princeton University, 1957). For an antidote to the crass oversimplification of my own procedures in this question, consult the

work of Georg Lukacs; e.g., "Das Nachher des rezeptiven Erlebnisses," *Ästhetik* (Berlin: Luchterhand, 1963), Part I, 835–51.

2. "Extracts from the Journal," March 12, 1870, pp. 121–23 in the Penguin edition (above, Chapter 5, n. 8). Compare also this from Cotton Mather:

> The anatomy of plants, as it has been exhibited by the incomparable curiosity of Dr. Grew—what a vast field of wonders does it lead us into!
> The most inimitable structure of the parts!
> The particular canals, and most adapted ones, for the conveyance of the lymphatic and essential juices!
> The air vessels in all their curious coilings!
> The coverings which befriend them, a work unspeakably more curious in reality than in appearance!
> The strange texture of the leaves, the angular or circular but always most orderly position of their fibres; the various foldings, with a duplicature, a multiplicature, the fore-roll, the back-roll, the tre-roll; the noble guard of the films interposed!
> The flowers, their gaiety and fragrancy; the perianthium or empalament of them; their curious foldings in the calyx before their expansion, with a close couch or a concave couch, a single plait or a double plait, or a plait and couch together, or a roll, or a spire, or plait and spire together; and their luxuriant colours after their foliation, and the expanding of their petala! (*The Christian Philosopher: A Collection of the Best Discoveries in Nature*, quoted in Carlo Izzo, *La letteratura nord-americana*, Florence and Milan: G. C. Sansoni and Edizioni Accademia, 1967, p. 36.)

3. For contrasting symphonic treatments of nature, one might begin with Ralph Vaughan Williams' *Pastoral Symphony*, symphonies 4–6 of Sibelius, and Mahler's *Third*, of which the composer wrote: "That this nature hides within itself everything that is frightful, great, and also lovely (which is exactly what I wanted to express in the entire work, in a sort of evolutionary development)—of course no one ever understands that. It always strikes me as odd that most people, when they speak of 'nature,' think only of flowers, little birds and woodsy smells. No one knows the god Dionysus, the great Pan" (Quoted and translated by Dika Newlin, *Bruckner, Mahler, Schoenberg*, New York: King's Crown, 1947, p. 121). The assumed naïve beatitude of his *Fourth Symphony* is, on the other hand, a very close analog to Longus, both in subject and in style.

4. For treatment of this topic from different perspectives, see Ben-

jamin Whorf, *Language, Thought, and Reality* (Cambridge, Mass.:
Massachusetts Institute of Technology, 1956), and Martin Heidegger,
Sein und Zeit (Tübingen: Neomarius, 1949), sect. 34, pp. 160–66—
or this, from the latter's *Einführung in die Metaphysik* (Tübingen:
Niemeyer, 1953), p. 11: "Words and language are not mere hulls, into
which things are packed for the speaking and writing market. Only in
the word, in language, do things come into being and be." For a full
tabulation of the various meanings of "nature" in antiquity, see Arthur
D. Lovejoy and George Boas, *Primitivism and Related Ideas in Antiquity* (Baltimore: Johns Hopkins, 1935).

    5. In his "Observations" prefixed to *Lyrical Ballads*.

    6. S. T. Coleridge, *Biographia Literaria*, ed. J. Shawcross (Oxford:
Clarendon, 1907), II, 39–40.

    7. J. R. R. Tolkien, "On Fairy Stories," *The Tolkien Reader* (New
York: Ballantine Books, 1966), pp. 70–73. From quite a different viewpoint, see Lukacs' discussion of the optimistic ending in socialist realism: *Wider den missverstandenen Realismus* (Hamburg: Claassen,
1958), p. 135. Ernst Bloch provides the most penetrating and far-
ranging treatment of the subject known to me, in his *Das Prinzip
Hoffnung*.

    8. Carol Gesner, "The Tempest as a Pastoral Romance," *Shake-
speare Quarterly*, X (1959), 531–39. Gesner's thesis is supported by
Frank Kermode (to whom I owe the reference) in Shakespeare, *The
Tempest*, ed. Frank Kermode (New York: Random House, 1964),
p. 172.

    9. See, for example, Paul Turner's "Introduction" to his translation
(above, Chapter 5, n. 11), p. 13, and Wolff (above, Chapter 3, n. 4),
pp. 452–55.

    10. Rilke gives another version of this conception—a version which
he regards as non-Christian:

Nature, the things we associate with and use, are provisional and per-
ishable; but, so long as we are here, they are our possession and our
friendship; sharers in our trouble and gladness, just as they have been
the confidants of our ancestors. Therefore, not only must all that is
here not be vilified or degraded, but, just because of that very provisionality they share with us, all these appearances and things should
be, in the most fervent sense, comprehended by us and transformed.
Transformed? Yes, for our task is to stamp this provisional, perishing
earth into ourselves so deeply, so painfully and passionately, that its
being may rise again, "invisibly," in us. *We are the bees of the Invisible. . . .* The earth has no other refuge except to become invisible: in
us, who, through one part of our nature, have a share in the Invisible,

or, at least, share-certificates, and can increase our holding in invisibility during our being here,—only in us can this intimate and enduring transformation of the visible into an invisible no longer dependent on visibility and tangibility be accomplished. . . . (Quoted and translated by J. B. Leishman in Rainer Maria Rilke, *Sonnets to Orpheus,* trans. J. B. Leishman, London: Hogarth, 1946, pp. 18–19.)

11. Rohde, p. 549.

12. Chalk, p. 49. An erotic-lascivious element not infrequently appears in ancient works of edifying religious intent. See Kerenyi (above, Chapter 6, n. 16), pp. 207ff.

13. The latter is, however, deserving of more attention than it receives. What with hippies and participantly democratic rebels, we are still deeply involved with the various aspects of Rousseau's message which it affectingly espouses. I should note here another remarkable emulation of *Daphnis and Chloe—The Sound of Waves,* by Yukio Mishima (trans. Meredith Weatherby, New York, 1956). I am indebted to my student Charles Myers for the reference to it and to a discussion of it by Frank Baldanza in "The Sound of Greek Waves in Japan," *The East-West Review* III 1 (Winter 1966–67), 66–82.

14. Together with Lolita, there should be a study of other "black" forms of the Romance pattern, such as *Les Liaisons Dangereuses,* and John Collier's *His Monkey Wife.*

15. Lindsay, p. 94.

16. Norman O. Brown, *Life Against Death: The Psychoanalytical Meaning of History* (Middletown, Conn.: Wesleyan University, 1959); *Love's Body* (New York: Random House, 1966).

17. Brown, *Life Against Death,* p. 93. Norman Brown may serve as a representative of the many current aspirations toward a post-technological health and simplicity, whether in the new politics inspired by Herbert Marcuse, or Walden-virtue, or Whitman-Ginsberg democratic-erotic mysticism.

18. For example:

But those who bewail the passing of the era in which this stable, idyllic condition was supposed to have obtained forget one important fact: only a tiny minority of people ever really enjoyed such pastoral permanence. The majority of people in premobile societies lived and worked in ways we would not want to return to. Most of us today would vigorously object to living in the house or doing the job our great-grandfathers did. The fact is that most people's great-grandparents were dirt-poor and lived in hovels. (Harvey Cox, *The Secular City: Secularization and Urbanization in Theological Perspective* [New York: Macmillan, 1965], p. 52.)

Contrast:

"I still think having a farm is a nice way to live," said Bishop Roy L. Schlabach of Holmes County. "You have a closer family life, your children work with you and working with nature keeps you closer to God." (Alma Kaufman, "Urbanization Is Forcing Amish to Give up Farms," reprinted from *Cleveland Plain Dealer* in *Mount Vernon News*, Mount Vernon, Ohio, June 30, 1967)

19. Lewis Mumford, *The Highway and the City* (New York: Harcourt, Brace, and World, 1963), p. 232.

20. For further discussion of the pastoral ideal as an active cultural principle and its importance in literature, see Leo Marx, *The Machine in the Garden: Technology and the Pastoral Ideal in America* (New York: Oxford University, 1964). On pastorality and city planning, see Lewis Mumford, "Suburbia and Beyond," *The City in History: Its Origins, Its Transformations, and Its Prospects* (New York: Harcourt, Brace, and World, 1961), and "Landscape and Townscape," *The Highway and the City* (above, n. 19).

21. Lindsay, p. 94. The link between standard Romance and the middle classes is also pointed out by Martin Braun, *History and Romance in Graeco-Oriental Literature* (Oxford: Blackwell, 1938), p. 11.

22. Quoted in Edgar Snow, *Red Star Over China* (New York: Random House, 1944), p. 128.

23. Georg Lukacs, *The Historical Novel*, trans. Hannah and Stanley Mitchell (London: Merlin, 1962), p. 348.

24. Compare the disagreement between Rilke and Rudolf Kassner on the value of time-involved selfhood—summarized by J. B. Leishman in his commentary on the Eighth "Duino Elegy" in Rainer Maria Rilke, *Duino Elegies*, trans. J. B. Leishman and Stephen Spender (London: Hogarth, 1952), pp. 132–35. The whole of the eighth elegy should be read in this connection—a rich and subtle variant treatment of life in nature as profoundly "idyllic" (although that word is inappropriate for Rilke).

25. "Certainly, town planning, city planning, conservation of natural and scenic resources are more in the spirit of socialism, even a despotic socialism, than in that of free enterprise." (Mary McCarthy, *The New York Review of Books*, Jan. 18, 1968, p. 8.) See also Edgar Snow, "The Yellow River Turns Blue," *The Other Side of the River: Red China Today* (New York: Random House, 1961).

26. *Quotations from Chairman Mao Tse-Tung*, introd. A. Doak Barnett (New York: Bantam Books, 1967), p. 17. If for some readers this is excessively strong meat, perhaps a transition could be mediated by the pessimist social critique of a much earlier, quite respectable pas-

toral poem—one which has had the sanction of generations of high-school English classes:

> Sweet smiling village, loveliest of the lawn,
> Thy sports are fled, and all thy charms withdrawn;
> Amidst thy bowers the tyrant's hand is seen,
> And desolation saddens all thy green:
> One only master grasps the whole domain.
> . . . .
> Ill fares the land, to hastening ills a prey,
> Where wealth accumulates, and men decay:
> . . . .
> . . . a bold peasantry, their country's pride,
> When once destroyed, can never be supplied.
> (from "The Deserted Village," Oliver Goldsmith)

27. Sigmund Freud, *Civilization and Its Discontents,* trans. Joan Riviere (New York: Cape, 1930).

28. In all my concluding discussion I do not mean to imply that there are not countless other ways in which *Daphnis and Chloe* falls short of being a compendium of truth about life. But one must in general allow a work to be what it sets out to be; utopianism, however, seems worth the special criticism of which I have here been making a preliminary—or derivative—sketch.

29. "Pleasure is Nature's test, her sign of approval. When man is happy, he is in harmony with himself and his environment. The new Individualism, for whose service Socialism, whether it wills it or not, is working, will be perfect harmony. It will be what the Greeks sought for, but could not, except in Thought, realise completely, because they had slaves, and fed them; it will be what the Renaissance sought for, but could not realise completely except in Art, because it had slaves, and starved them. It will be complete, and through it each man will attain to his perfection. The new Individualism is the new Hellenism." (Oscar Wilde, "The Soul of Man under Socialism" [above, Chapter 5, n. 3], V, 64–65.)

To carry the fancy further: in our part of the present century, among the various literary stances conceivable for a modern Longus, one could for example picture him as aligned with (non-revolutionary, hence idyllic) literary conservationists such as Louis Bromfield, Anne Morrow Lindbergh, and Rachel Carson.

Selected Bibliography

I have included only those works which I have been able to consult. (See Preface, n. 1, for some omissions.) Schönberger's edition of the Greek text (see below) provides a very full bibliography for *Daphnis and Chloe* alone; Perry's *The Ancient Romances* (see below under "Studies of Greek Romance in General") gives a useful annotated bibliography for Romance generally. For general reference, see *Oxford Classical Dictionary;* Pauly-Wissowa, *Realenzyklopädie der klassischen Altertumswissenschaft;* W. Schmid and others, *Geschichte der griechischen Literatur;* W. H. Roscher, *Ausführliches Lexicon der griechischen und römischen Mythologie.* For annual bibliography, including articles and reviews, see J. Marouzeau, *L'Année philologique.*

Greek Text with Introduction, Notes, and Translation

Daphnis and Chloe, trans. George Thornley, ed. J. M. Edmonds. London: William Heinemann; New York: G. P. Putnam's Sons (Loeb Classical Library), 1916. Text outmoded. Translation "revised" into Latin at touchy moments.

Hirtengeschichten von Daphnis und Chloe, ed. and trans. Otto Schönberger. Berlin: Akademie-Verlag, 1960. The most important single work on *Daphnis and Chloe.* A marvel of condensed, comprehensive discussion and information. Eight plates.

Pastorales (Daphnis et Chloé), ed. and trans. Georges Dalmeyda. Paris: "Les Belles Lettres," 2d ed. 1960. Valuable introduction and notes.

Translations Alone

AMYOT, J., trans., *Daphnis et Chloé.* Paris: V. Sertenas, 1559. This famous version, constantly reprinted, established the popularity of Longus throughout Europe, almost forty years before the first publication of the Greek text (in 1598). Some have preferred it to the original.

DAYE, ANGELL, trans., *Daphnis and Chloe: excellently describing the weight of affection, the simplicitie of love, the purport of honest meaning, the resolution of men, and disposition of Fate, finished in a Pastorall, and interlaced with the praises of a most peerlesse Princesse, wonderfull in Maiestie, and rare in perfection, celebrated within the same Pastorall, and therefore termed by the name of The Shepheards Holidaie.* London: Robert Waldegrave, 1587. Reprinted and edited by Joseph Jacobs, London, 1890. A charming, willfully free version (not based on the Greek text) which omits an entire sequence of the plot and substitutes a pastoral celebration of Queen Elizabeth.

HADAS, MOSES, trans., in *Three Greek Romances*. Garden City, N.Y., Doubleday and Co., 1953. Attempts a close rendering. Result: sluggish.

LINDSAY, JACK, trans., *Daphnis and Chloe*. London: Daimon, 1948. Lindsay seeks out bright words and vivid phrases, so far as his fidelity to the text will permit. Should be given a reprint in paperback.

MOORE, GEORGE, trans., *The Pastoral Loves of Daphnis and Chloe*. New York: Limited Editions Club, 1934. Moore's introduction is worth reading for its own sake: a portrait of the jaded author revivified by his discovery of Longus. The translation is based on the French of Courier; it is beautiful, but the beauty is not current.

PETIT-RADEL, P., trans., *Longi Sophistae Pastoralia Lesbiaca sive De Amoribus Daphnidis et Chloes: Poema Erotico-Poimenicon e Textu Graeco in Latinum Numeris Heroicis Deductum*. Paris: Agasse/Bertrand, 1809. In addition to his version in Latin Hexameters, Petit-Radel provides one in Latin prose, and a verbose Latin preface. I cite this pleasant curio here since it seems to have slipped past even the zealously bibliographic Schönberger.

THORNLEY, GEORGE, trans., *Daphnis and Chloe: A Most Sweet and Pleasant Pastoral Romance for Young Ladies*. London: John Garfield, 1657. Free and pleasing; probably the best in English, but too old to be Longus' English ambassador. Often reprinted. Of particular interest: Pantheon, 1949, with woodcuts by Aristide Maillol.

TURNER, PAUL, trans., *Daphnis and Chloe*. Penguin Books, 1956. Fresh and readable, but no aroma. Good brief introduction.

Translations of Other Greek Romances

ACHILLES TATIUS. *The Adventures of Leucippe and Clitophon*, ed. and trans. S. Gaselee. London: William Heinemann; New York: G. P. Putnam's Sons (Loeb Classical Library), 1917.

CHARITON. *Chaereas and Callirhoe*, trans. Warren E. Blake. Ann Arbor: University of Michigan, 1939.

HELIODORUS. *An Ethiopian Tale,* trans. Moses Hadas. Ann Arbor: University of Michigan, 1957.

XENOPHON OF EPHESUS. *An Ephesian Tale,* in *Three Greek Romances,* trans. Moses Hadas. Garden City, N.Y.: Doubleday and Company, 1953.

Studies of Daphnis and Chloe Alone

CHALK, H. H. O. "Eros and the Lesbian Pastorals of Longos," *Journal of Hellenic Studies,* LXXX (1960), 32–51. Second only to Schönberger's edition in its value; 1960 was Longus' year, it seems.

FRANCE, ANATOLE. "Daphnis et Chloé," *Le genie Latin,* pp. 1–8. Paris: Alphonse Lemerre, 1913. Originally a preface to a translation. Inaccuracies, but a charming, shrewd sense for Longus' decadent artifice.

LINDSAY, JACK. "Critical Essay," appendix to his translation (see above). Some irrelevant material, some erratic judgment; otherwise a worthy forerunner to Chalk's exposition.

MERKELBACH, REINHOLD. "Daphnis und Chloe: Roman und Mysterium," *Antaios,* I (1960), 47–60. Boldly but often persuasively develops the role of late Dionysian mystery-cult themes in Longus. (Note once more the *annus mirabilis* 1960.)

MITTELSTADT, MICHAEL CHARLES. "Longus and the Greek Love Romance." Dissertation, Stanford University, 1964 (University Microfilms). A careful study of Longus' pastoral originality compared with standard Romance. Despite apparent disregard of Chalk's work, it develops important new insights on the "education" of Daphnis and Chloe, and on the stylistic relation between Longus and contemporary narrative painting. (See n. 13 to Chapter 5, pp. 124f.)

ROHDE, GEORG. "Longus und die Bukolik," *Rheinisches Museum für Philologie,* LXXXVI (1937), 23–49. A very important study. In addition to his close examination of Longus' transformation of the pastoral poets, G. Rohde was apparently the first to delineate the specifically pastoral *religious* basis of the work.

VALLEY, GUNNAR. *Über den Sprachgebrauch des Longus.* Uppsala: Berling, 1926. Exhaustive examination of Longus' diction and syntax; extensive list of passages influenced by previous authors.

Studies of Greek Romance in General

ALTHEIM, FRANZ. *Roman und Dekadenz.* Tübingen: Niemeyer, 1951. The ancient and modern novel as symptomatic of a cultural phase; accepts much of Kerènyi's orientation (see below).

BRAUN, MARTIN. *History and Romance in Graeco-Oriental Literature.* Oxford: Blackwell, 1938. The influence on Romance of national patriotic legends in countries subject to Hellenistic rule.

CALDERINI, ARISTIDE. "Prolegomeni," in Caritone di Afrodisia, *Le avventure di Cherea e Callirhoe,* trans. Aristide Calderini. Turin, 1913. Thorough analyses of pervasive characteristics of the Romances.

HAIGHT, ELIZABETH HAZELTON. *Essays on the Greek Romances.* Port Washington, N.Y.: Kennikat, 1965 (1st ed., 1943). Useful profiles of the individual works.

HELM, RUDOLF, *Der antike Roman.* Göttingen: Vandenhoek und Ruprecht, 1956, 2d ed. Chiefly taken up with plot summaries of the ancient novels in all categories and useful for its comprehensiveness in this respect; brief assessments of most novels appended.

KERÉNYI, KARL. *die Griechisch-Orientalische Romanliteratur in religionsgeschichtlicher Beleuchtung: Ein Versuch.* Tübingen: J. C. B. Mohr (Paul Siebeck), 1927. Like Rohde's book (below), a work of overwhelming scholarship. The derivation of Romance from the cults of Isis and related Oriental divinities is too narrow and cranky, but the enrichment of the religious context of the Romances is immense. (I have not seen Merkelbach's recent book of similar tendency—see Preface, n. 1.)

LAVAGNINI, BRUNO. *Studi sul Romanzo Greco.* Messina and Florence: G. d'Anna, 1950. Includes the author's *Le Origini del Romanzo Greco* (1921). Derives Romance from the historiographic transformation of local legends and myths. Particularly useful discussion of papyrological fragments.

PERRY, BEN EDWIN. *The Ancient Romances: A Literary-Historical Account of Their Origins.* Berkeley and Los Angeles: University of California, 1967. Currently the most important book on the subject.

ROHDE, ERWIN. *Der griechische Roman und seine Vorläufer,* 4th ed., Hildesheim: Olms, 1960. Despite the invalidation of its central thesis, the richness and power of the treatment in detail will preserve this as the scholarly classic in the field.

SCHMID, WILHELM, and OTTO STÄHLIN. *Wilhelm von Christs Geschichte der griechischen Literatur,* 6th ed., Part II, second half. Munich: Beck, 1924. Condensed but thorough discussion of all ancient novels, with abundant scholarly references.

SCHWARTZ, EDUARD. *Fünf Vorträge über den griechischen Roman: Das Romanhafte in der erzählenden Literatur der Griechen,* 2d ed. Berlin: Walter de Gruyter, 1943 (1st ed., 1896). By way of a brilliantly evocative survey of the Romantic tendencies in an-

cient historiography and other narratives, develops a position
partially ancestral to Lavagnini (see above). Very little direct
discussion of the Romances, however.

TODD, F. A. *Some Ancient Novels.* London, 1940. Separate essays of
an introductory sort.

TRENKNER, SOPHIE. *The Greek Novella in the Classical Period.* Cambridge University, 1958. Although not directly concerned with
Romance, of great value for the understanding of narrative forms
and themes prior to Romance.

WEINREICH, OTTO. *Der griechische Liebesroman.* Zürich: Artemis,
1962. For the erotic Romances, a brilliant little jewel: lively,
informative, compressed; special attention to Heliodoros.

WOLFF, SAMUEL LEE. *The Greek Romances in Elizabethan Prose
Fiction.* New York, 1912. Valuable also for its treatment of the
ancient Romances per se.

Studies of the Pastoral and the Pastoral Tradition

CLARK, KENNETH. "Ideal Landscape," Chapter IV of *Landscape into
Art.* Boston: Beacon, 1961 (first published, 1949). The pastoral
mode in painting from the Renaissance to the nineteenth century.

EMPSON, WILLIAM. *Some Versions of Pastoral.* Norfolk, Conn.: New
Directions, 1960 (first published, London, 1936). A famous
formulation and versatile extension of the pastoral idea beyond
nominally pastoral literature.

GRANT, W. LEONARD. *Neo-Latin Literature and the Pastoral.* Chapel
Hill, N.C.: University of North Carolina, 1965. Surveys a narrow
but crowded field; very full bibliography, including the pastoral
generally.

KERMODE, FRANK, ed., *English Pastoral Poetry from the Beginnings to
Marvell.* London: Harrap, 1952. Includes a good introductory
essay.

LAWALL, GILBERT. *Theocritus' Coan Pastorals: A Poetry Book.* Cambridge, Mass.: Harvard University, 1967. This should revolu-
tionize the understanding of Theokritos. In revealing thematic
issues and symbols, Lawall overthrows the conventional doctrine
that Theokritos was merely a "genre painter."

MARX, LEO. *The Machine in the Garden: Technology and the Pastoral
Ideal in America.* New York: Oxford University, 1964. A brilliant
documentation of the creative but problematic vitality of the
pastoral as a continuing force in the literary and cultural imagination. The most important book known to me on the pastoral.

OTIS, BROOKS. "The Young Virgil," Chapter IV in *Virgil: A Study in
Civilized Poetry.* Oxford: Clarendon, 1963. The finest discussion
of Vergil's contribution to pastoral literature.

PANOFSKY, ERWIN. "*Et in Arcadia ego:* Poussin and the Elegiac Tradition," Chapter VII in *Meaning and the Visual Arts*. Garden City, N.Y.: Doubleday and Company, 1957. A fascinating sidepath in the exploration of pastoral themes.

PÖSCHL, VIKTOR. *Die Hirtendichtung Virgils*. Heidelberg: Winter, 1964. An extremely penetrating study of two of Vergil's *Eclogues*.

SNELL, BRUNO. "Arcadia: The Discovery of a Spiritual Landscape," Chapter XIII in *The Discovery of the Mind: The Greek Origins of European Thought*, trans. T. G. Rosenmeyer. New York: Harper, 1960 (first published in English, 1953). Profound treatment of Vergil's divergence from Theokritos.

N.B.: One of the superabundant merits of Schönberger's edition is its extremely thorough précis of Longus' influence up to the present in literature, plastic arts, and music (see above, under "Greek Text with Introduction, Notes, and Translation").

Utopias in Literature and Society

BLOCH, ERNST. *Das Prinzip Hoffnung*, 2 vols. Frankfurt am Main: Suhrkamp, 1959. A monumental study of the teleological orientation of human life, written from a highly individualist Marxist viewpoint, incorporating a comprehensive theory of utopian and other ideal imagination.

Utopia: Daedalus, Spring, 1965. Essays on many aspects of the subject, from a variety of contributors. See especially Northrop Frye, "Varieties of Literary Utopias," pp. 323–47.

FINLEY, MOSES I. "Utopianism Ancient and Modern," in *The Critical Spirit: Essays in Honor of Herbert Marcuse*, eds. Kurt H. Wolff and Barrington Moore, Jr. Boston: Beacon: 1967. A brief essay of great interest.

LOVEJOY, ARTHUR O. and GEORGE BOAS. *Primitivism and Related Ideas in Antiquity*. Baltimore: Johns Hopkins, 1935. An extremely valuable basic collection of sources and discussion of utopian and other theories of "the simple life" in antiquity.

Index

Achilleus Tatios, 24, 33, 39, 41, 60, 65, 66–67, 68, 79, 80, 87
Aelian, 42, 43, 58
Aeneid (Vergil), 30, 64
Aeschylus, 115
Alexander the Great, 29; biographies of, 28, 32
Alkaios, 74
Alkiphron, 58, 59, 87
Amaltheia, 88
Amyot, 61
Anakreon, 96
Aphrodite, 22, 28, 75
Apuleius, 80, 82, 99
Arcadia, 55, 57, 74, 101–102
Aristophanes, 30, 47; *Birds*, 85; *Peace*, 47
Aristotle, 26, 103; *Poetics*, 27
Arrowsmith, William, 40
Artemis, 25, 81
Asianism, 37–38
Asklepiades, 77
Astylos, 19, 57, 58, 93
Atticism, 38, 58
Auerbach, Erich, *Mimesis*, 30, 80
Augustine, S., 79

Bakchai (Euripides), 95, 96–97
Barth, John, 62
Baudelaire, Charles, 79
Beethoven, L. von, *Pastoral Symphony*, 108
Bion, 71, 98
Birds (Aristophanes), 85
Bloch, Ernst, 114
Brown, N. O., 112–113

Chaireas, 22, 23, 27
Chalk, H. H. O., 32, 65, 81, 85, 88, 111–112
Chariton, 22–23, 27, 31, 35, 68
Chloe, significance of name, 83; *et passim.*
Cicero, 103
Coleridge, S. T., 109
Comedy, New, 28, 48, 57–59, 64, 67, 88, 93, 114
Comedy, Roman, 114
Cox, Harvey, 113
Cynics, 33, 43
Cyrus, 32

d'Anse de Villoison, 60
Dante, 102, 111, 115
Daphnis, in Theokritos I, 53; significance of name, 83; *et passim*
Day, Angel, 61
Demeter, 84
Demosthenes, 39
de Saint-Pierre, Bernardin, *Paul et Virginie*, 112
Dion of Prusa, *Euboean Discourse*, 33, 34, 43, 102
Dionysophanes, 19, 67, 86, 87, 88, 89, 93, 114; significance of name, 84
Dionysos, 32, 66, 81, 84, 85, 86, 88, 90, 91, 92, 95, 96–97
Dorkon, 16, 41, 49, 54, 63, 64, 67, 92, 95
Dryas, 15, 18, 19, 70, 92, 117; significance of name, 84, 88
Dyskolos (Menander), 57–58, 59, 63

139

Passages Quoted from Daphnis and Chloe

Ancient Authors Quoted

Modern Authors Quoted